Conversations with John le Carré

Literary Conversations Series

Peggy Whitman Prenshaw
General Editor

Conversations with John le Carré

Edited by
Matthew J. Bruccoli and Judith S. Baughman

University Press of Mississippi
Jackson

www.upress.state.ms.us

The University Press of Mississippi is a member of the Association of American University Presses.

12 11 10 09 08 07 06 05 04   4 3 2 1

∞

Library of Congress Cataloging-in-Publication

Le Carré, John, 1931–
  Conversations with John le Carré / edited by Matthew J. Bruccoli and Judith S. Baughman.
    p. cm.
  Includes index.
  ISBN 1-57806-668-9 (cloth : alk. paper) — ISBN 1-57806-669-7 (pbk. : alk. paper)
  1. Le Carré, John, 1931– —Interviews. 2. Psychological fiction, English—History and criticism—Theory, etc. 3. Spy stories, English—History and criticism—Theory, etc. 4. Novelists, English—20th century—Interviews. 5. Psychological fiction—Authorship. 6. Spy stories—Authorship. 7. Cold War in literature. I. Bruccoli, Matthew Joseph, 1931– II. Baughman, Judith. III. Title.
  PR6062.E33Z466 2004
  823'.914—dc22   2004009379

British Library Cataloging-in-Publication Data available

Books by John le Carré

A Call for the Dead. London: Gollancz, 1961; New York: Walker, 1962.

A Murder of Quality. London: Gollancz, 1962; New York: Walker, 1963.

The Spy Who Came in From the Cold. London: Gollancz, 1963; New York: Coward-McCann, 1964.

The Looking-Glass War. London: Heinemann, 1965; New York: Coward-McCann, 1965.

A Small Town in Germany. London: Heinemann, 1968; New York: Coward-McCann, 1968.

The Naive and Sentimental Lover. London: Hodder & Stoughton, 1971; New York: Knopf, 1972.

Tinker, Tailor, Soldier, Spy. London: Hodder & Stoughton, 1974; New York: Knopf, 1974.

The Honourable Schoolboy. London: Hodder & Stoughton, 1977; New York: Knopf, 1977.

Smiley's People. London: Hodder & Stoughton, 1980; New York: Knopf, 1980.

The Quest for Karla: Tinker, Tailor, Soldier, Spy; The Honourable Schoolboy; Smiley's People. New York: Knopf, 1982.

The Little Drummer Girl. New York: Knopf, 1983; London: Hodder & Stoughton, 1983.

A Perfect Spy. London: Hodder & Stoughton, 1986; New York: Knopf, 1986.

The Clandestine Muse. Portland, Oregon: Seluzicki, 1986.

The Russia House. London: Hodder & Stoughton, 1989; New York: Knopf, 1989.

The Secret Pilgrim. London: Hodder & Stoughton, 1991; New York: Knopf, 1991.

The Night Manager. London: Hodder & Stoughton, 1993; New York: Knopf, 1993.

Our Game. London: Hodder & Stoughton, 1995; New York: Knopf, 1995.

The Tailor of Panama. London: Hodder & Stoughton, 1996; New York: Knopf, 1996.

Single & Single. London: Hodder & Stoughton, 1999; New York: Scribner 1999; Toronto: Viking, 1999.

Sarratt and the Draper of Watford by John le Carré and Other Unlikely Stories about Sarratt from International Authors. No place: no publisher, [1999].

The Constant Gardener. London: Hodder & Stoughton, 2001; New York: Scribner, 2001.

Absolute Friends. London: Hodder & Stoughton, 2004; New York: Little Brown, 2004.

Principal Books about le Carré

Aronoff, Myron J. *The Spy Novels of John le Carré*. New York: St. Martin's Press, 1999.

Beene, Lynn Dianne. *John le Carré*. New York: Twayne, 1992.

Bloom, Harold, ed. *John le Carré*. New York: Chelsea House, 1987.

Bold, Alan, ed. *The Quest for le Carré*. London: Vision Press, 1998; New York: St. Martin's Press, 1998.

Cobbs, John L. *Understanding John le Carré*. Columbia: University of South Carolina Press, 1998.

Homberger, Eric. *John le Carré*. London & New York: Methuen, 1986.

Lewis, Peter. *John le Carré*. New York: Ungar, 1985.

Monaghan, David. *The Novels of John le Carré: The Art of Survival*. Oxford: Blackwell, 1985.

Monaghan. *Smiley's Circus*. New York: St. Martin's Press, 1986.

Wolfe, Peter. *Corridors of Deceit: The World of John le Carré*. Bowling Green, Ohio: Bowling Green Popular Press, 1987.

For George Greenfield

Contents

Introduction

The Spy Novel is a British genre. If they didn't invent it, they perfected it. The stable of twentieth-century British masters includes Eric Ambler, John Buchan, Joseph Conrad, Len Deighton, early Ian Fleming, Frederick Forsyth, Graham Greene, William Haggard, Geoffrey Household, Somerset Maugham, and John le Carré. Americans aren't very good at it, except for Charles McCarry and Alan Furst. The disparity—at least before the Cold War—may be accounted for by the English tradition of the gentleman amateur: the patriot who serves England out of a sense of public-school privilege. There is a distinct element of snobbery in the classic British spy novels.

One way to differentiate the British and American schools is that most of the best British spy novels are about class, as is most of British fiction. The best British spy novels provide social history as well as international or political history. This claim is supported by David Cornwell's recordings of his books: he does the Brits in different voices.

The term "category fiction"—applied condescendingly—probably began as an American publishing term to identify the categories of titles that had to be supplied for the paperback racks: westerns, mysteries, sci-fi, romance. Spy novels, originally lumped with the mysteries, grew into their own category. In Britain spy novels are known as "thrillers," an amorphous category that includes mystery/crime/suspense fiction—but not the murder-in-the-country-cottage whodunits knows as "cosies."

World Wars I and II stimulated the writing of spy novels, and the Cold War had a strong influence on their publication and material. The boom was launched in 1954 by Ian Fleming's *Casino Royale* and *To Live and Let Die*; but Fleming degenerated into profitable self-parody that cheapened the genre. Richard Clayton, a government official writing as William Haggard, preceded David Cornwell/John le Carré with *Slow Burner* (1958), *The Telemann Touch* (1958), *Venetian Blind* (1959), *The Closed Circuit* (1960), and *The Arena* (1961). He published thirty-five novels with diminishing success. The initial favorable reception of his early books was spoiled by the critical reaction against Haggard's high Toryism, and his books are undeservedly buried.

David Cornwell, writing as John le Carré published two slim apprentice novels, *A Call for the Dead* (1962) and *A Murder of Quality* (1963) before the great success of *The Spy Who Came in From the Cold* (1964). Len Deighton published *The Ipcress File* (1964) and *Funeral in Berlin* (1965) and continues to write spy novels, but he has not achieved the standing of le Carré.

The chief impediment to the proper assessment of spy novels, as well as other category novels, is that it takes time for them to overcome their sub-literary standing, as with the now-classic American hard-boiled novels. Of the British spy novelists now writing, le Carré has been accorded the most respect as a literary figure—but with reservations. It is a commonplace observation that his literary position has been damaged by his material and that he would be regarded as a more significant figure if he had written about something else; but his only "straight" novel *The Naive and Sentimental Lover* (1971) flopped with readers and critics. Writers don't pick their material: it picks them. Thus F. Scott Fitzgerald's complaints about *The Great Gatsby*: "But, my God! It was my material, and it was all I had to deal with." It is sufficient that le Carré writes superlatively well about his material.

Le Carré's popular reputation was promoted by speculation about his own career as a spy, which he at first denied or minimized in interviews. This angle was gradually overshadowed by his revelations about his con-man father, who indoctrinated him into the world of deception. Ronnie Cornwell runs through his son's novels more or less disguised, and openly in *A Perfect Spy* (1986), the best le Carré novel.

It is proper to address the question of the utility of the le Carré interviews assembled here—indeed, of author interviews in general. The tests are whether they increase the reader's understanding of the works and whether the interviews are worth reading in themselves as oral literature. The difficulty in assessing the usability and reliability of any interview is that the reader normally has no knowledge of the interviewer's trustworthiness or animus. A couple of le Carré's interviewers seem to resent his income. Some interviewers regard the assignment as an opportunity to reveal their own literary skills. The most serious flaw in the interview as a form of autobiography is that the subject almost never has the opportunity to check the prepublication text for accuracy—assuming that he offers to do so. In America such requests are perceived as violations of the reporter's First Amendment right to get it wrong. Even careful interviewers may have their work tampered with by editors.

David Cornwell/John le Carré—sometimes it is difficult to determine which of them is speaking—is adept at handling interviewers. He eschews irony. He answers the questions seriously, even when they are the same questions that other interviewers have asked. He never commits the blunder of making interviewers feel dumb. Like other celebrity writers, he has developed protective techniques for giving interviewers what they can use, without telling them anything they can use against him.

Editorial Note

The spelling of David Cornwell's by-line has been regularized to John le Carré. Some of the interviewers' redundant headnotes have been cut.

MJB
JSB

Chronology

1931	19 October: David John Moore Cornwell, second son of Ronald and Olive Glassy Cornwell, born in Poole, Dorset.
1934–1935	Ronald Cornwell imprisoned for fraud; Olive Cornwell deserts her family.
1948	David Cornwell leaves Sherborne School and attends Bern University in Switzerland for a year.
1950–1952	Cornwell is drafted; serves in British army intelligence in Vienna.
1952–1954	Cornwell studies modern languages at Lincoln College, Oxford.
1954	Cornwell marries Alison Ann Veronica Sharp. Ronald Cornwell goes bankrupt. David Cornwell leaves Oxford to teach at Millfield Junior School during 1954–1955.
1955–1956	Cornwell returns to Oxford and graduates with a first-class degree.
1956–1958	Cornwell teaches languages at Eton.
1958–1960	Cornwell works as freelance illustrator; is possibly employed by MI5 (British Security Service).
1960–1963	Cornwell works for the British Foreign Office in Bonn; possibly employed by MI6 (British Secret Intelligence Service).
1961	Cornwell adopts pseudonym John le Carré with the publication of his first novel, *A Call for the Dead*.
1962	Publication of *A Murder of Quality*.
1963	Cornwell is transferred by Foreign Office to Hamburg. Publication of *The Spy Who Came in From the Cold*, a critical and popular success.
1965	Cornwell resigns from Foreign Office; becomes full-time writer. Publication of *The Looking-Glass War*.
1968	Publication of *A Small Town in Germany*.
1971	Publication of *The Naive and Sentimental Lover*. Divorce.

Conversations with John le Carré

John le Carré: The Writer, like the Spy, Is an Illusionist

Véra Volmane / 1965

Reprinted from *Les Nouvelles Litteraires*, 23 September 1965, p. 3. Copyright © *Les Nouvelles Litteraires*. Translated by Cristy S. Vogel.

At thirty, John le Carré acquired world renown for The Spy Who Came in From the Cold: *seventeen million copies sold. Physically, he shares a likeness with Richard Burton (the actor who incarnated Leamas[1] who "came in from the cold" in the motion-picture adaptation of the novel): a face with somewhat blurred contours that reveal a certain vulnerability despite the confidence in his voice. As a former civil servant at the Foreign Office, he manages to maintain good manners, infallible courtesy, and an accent that makes all of the citizens of Oxford in the United Kingdom pale with jealousy.*

Interviewer: Why this liking for a tragic end? Your *Looking-Glass War* ends as badly as your previous book.

le Carré: The men of whom I speak are already condemned: they are finished, worn-out; their emotional experiences were dulled during the war. They are the last of a lost generation; they need young people to take over in order to find themselves, reflecting in a mirror: Avery[2] is their last chance. The material that I have chosen extrapolates the theme of espionage. I attempted to illustrate the paradox of war. It sacrifices the individual in the battle against collectivity, which is absurd. It was Montesquieu who said that never have there been as many wars as in the kingdom of Christ. And in *The Looking-Glass War*, Avery faces all sorts of problems.

Interviewer: Where does this pessimism come from?

le Carré: From my observations.

---

1. Alec Leamas, protagonist of le Carré's break-through novel.
2. John Avery, character in *The Looking-Glass War*.

Interviewer: So you describe an observed reality?
le Carré: In a sense, yes. At the Foreign Office, I worked in an "orthodox" department; I didn't deal with the spies. At the Foreign Affairs Office, as at Eton where I taught, I noticed a sort of obsession that everybody seemed to have: we looked for our identity in history and in the justification of power.

Interviewer: Does the past explain the present?
le Carré: No, these are ghosts that we must fight.

Interviewer: Do you believe that it's better to fight them with unpleasant characters?
le Carré: Are they unpleasant? They aren't good, but for reasons that I can sympathize with. They are incapable of making a decision. They must obey. Leamas is destructive out of weakness, out of a spirit of revenge. But above all because he's a man of action in a world of confused ideologies.

Interviewer: Have you been beyond the Iron Curtain?
le Carré: Never. I had some interviews with emigrants, some refugees.

Interviewer: Do you think that your vision of the communist world conforms to reality?
le Carré: Certainly not, since the majority of my characters behave as men from the western world who would have come to Communism as an antidote to the western way of life. It seems to me that the system is too fair; it is almost carried out according to principles of Roman law. It's the type of system that we could have if we were communists.

Interviewer: Explain the difference you make between "us" and "them"?
le Carré: Them, these are the men of the political East. Their problems aren't familiar to us. We have been brought up in the western spirit, and it's perhaps the weakness of the spy, an inevitable weakness since I'm not familiar with the world that I describe.

Interviewer: Your novels draw on invention then?
le Carré: I exercised my imagination, and I don't care if this doesn't correspond to reality, as long as the plot maintains its credibility. It doesn't matter

to me if Daudet does or doesn't go to Africa with Tartarian, if Kipling has or hasn't been to India, if Balzac has or hasn't explored Paris—as long as I believe what they said.

Interviewer: But the profound reason that pushed you to write these spy novels?
le Carré: I fear that I cannot answer this question. I had to choose the world of spies because it illustrates what I had to say: the solitude of the designated victim.

Interviewer: In the sense that you give to the word "victim," isn't he or she always lonely?
le Carré: I would like to think not. A spy, like a writer, lives outside the mainstream population. He steals his experience through bribes and reconstructs it. The writer, like the spy, is an illusionist. He creates images that he finds within himself; he illustrates his universe with words from this immense world.

Interviewer: If you were to meet a real spy who would tell you how things really are, would you take it into account?
le Carré: Surely not. It has already been done: in the United States, I was approached by a young man who told me that he worked for the CIA. He told me how my stories were not true. What does it matter? In the German publication *Der Spiegel*, the person who was "second in command" of the West German secret services published an article on my first novel: "Nichts ist authentisch" [Nothing is authentic]. I answered him in German in the same newspaper. Only my title was in English: "A cat is a secret dog." There are a lot of examples in the past where the German secret services lost quite a bit of time and trouble trying to distinguish unsuccessfully between fact and fiction. I hope that this gentleman will have read Kafka attentively and will be able to confirm that such a case never took place in the East. He will probably be right. The fact remains that my books stay true and real for me. There are several ways for a novelist to be the witness of his time.

Interviewer: Like Mérimée with *Les chants de la Guzla* and Goethe with *Ossian*, in retrospect, don't you want to go visit the countries of the East?
le Carré: It is much more than a wish, and I have expressed my desire to go to the U.S.S.R. Unfortunately, my request has not been answered.

The Fictional World of Espionage

Leigh Crutchley / 1966

Reprinted from *The Listener*, 75 (14 April 1966), 548–49. Copyright © *The Listener*. From an impromptu discussion on the BBC Home Service. Reprinted by permission.

Interviewer: Despite the fact that you have been compared with other writers on espionage, Mr. le Carré, you have your own style. Where did this style spring from?

le Carré: If you mean literary style, I think in part simply from the discipline both of teaching and of being a bureaucrat. One of the principles of Foreign Office drafting, whether you draft a telegram or whether you draft a despatch from your Ambassador, is that the smallest worm in the outfit tries to reflect what he hopes will be the Ambassador's opinion on a given subject. This is done out on blue paper with triple or quadruple spacing. This piece of paper or this sheaf of paper then works its way up through all his colleagues until it reaches the highest authority—in this case the Ambassador—and each of these wretched people adds his comments, eliminates loose words, questions style, questions the line of thought, until finally when it reaches the Ambassador he makes his own alterations and then it comes all the way down again. So that if one had any thoughts about the glories of one's prose style or any thoughts about the lucidity of one's argument, one was soundly disillusioned by the time the piece of paper came back. This made one wary, economic; it is certainly the most rigid, the most astringent training that I have had. I suppose you could say I got my style from there.

Interviewer: But your style goes deeper than this. You have developed what I suppose we can best describe as the anti-hero, haven't you?

le Carré: I don't quite believe in the notion of the anti-hero. George Orwell once said that we either write for the hero or the victim. You could translate that in modern terms into the difference between the literature of escapism and the literature of involvement. In the literature of escapism we have really run to two different kinds of hero. If one could subdivide that particular paragraph, we have had in the past the Sandy Arbuthnots, the Buchan figures,[1] the Geoffrey Household[2] figures who act within the realm of a discernible ethic, who are defending a society which we know and understand—the upper-middle-class society of England and the whole tradition of power which we have had. Since then something else has emerged, something very interesting. That is the James Bond kind of hero. I call this the consumer-goods hero.

This is the man who surrounds himself with all the things which are technique—with the charms of super cars, super and expendable girls, with cigarette lighters that go off with a bang, with everything which in artistic terms replaces love or emotion. You could take James Bond on that magic carpet and, given the prerequisites of the affluent society, given above all an identifiable villain of whatever kind—and weak people need enemies—you could dump him in the middle of Moscow and you would get a ready-made Soviet agent. I find him in this sense extremely cosmopolitan. He is an Etonian and so on, but in fact he seems to me to correspond more to the kind of international manager type—the young rich fellow of thirty-eight or thirty-nine who has discovered that promiscuity is one of the privileges of wealth; who has developed a pretty hard-nosed cynicism towards any sense of moral obligation.

This is, I think, an unconscious but pretty accurate reflection of some of the worst things in western society. And it will soon reflect on the worst things in eastern society. What I tried to do was to remake a figure who was involved in the dilemma of our time: that we cannot continue with the war epic. In the past we have shown that war was a legitimate means of self-defence or even, when we were empire building, a legitimate means of aggression. Now we have got the big bomb instead. We have not got an identifiable enemy; we have an ideology instead with which we must come to terms, and it seemed to me that the western dilemma of the small man is that the institutions we create to combat the ideology to fight the Cold War are getting so big that the individual himself is losing his identity in our society, just as he is in eastern society.

---

1. John Buchan (1875–1940), British author of espionage novels including *The Thirty-Nine Steps* (1915) and *Greenmantle* (1916). Sandy Arbuthnot was the hero of *Greenmantle*.
2. Geoffrey Household (1900–1988), British author of *Rouge Male* (1939) and other thrillers.

We have always argued that in the West we may be amorphous, we may be vague, we may contain a great variety of beliefs, but the one thing we have in common in a non-communist world is supposed to be the belief that the individual is worth more than the idea: that whatever we believe in, we will defend to the death the individual's right to dissent; and yet in the Cold War, and particularly in the spy world which is after all the battlefield of the Cold War, we are doing something *in fact* which I believe we are already doing *in principle* elsewhere—that is to say, we are sacrificing the individual in our battle against the collective. This is the supreme paradox. I want people when they open my book and begin ready to feel "God, this could be me!" When they are reading this other type of heroic book, I think they are saying "Oh, gosh, I wish this were me," and that is a sharp difference. Both may be, in long-haired terms, pop art, but I believe that mine at the moment has more application to our dilemma than the other.

Interviewer: In other words, you say that what we are doing on this sort of spy front is fighting the enemy with its own weapons?
le Carré: It is fighting the enemy with its own weapons, fighting fire with fire. I don't think that writers should be philosophers. I don't think that they should be too conscious of where they belong, but at least they do have, if they have a duty at all, the duty to explain to us what we are doing in the old words, to hold up some kind of mirror. I think we are doing this on a big scale when C.I.A. starts revolutions or wrecks a summit conference with the U2; we are doing it perhaps on a small scale when we recruit minor informants. We are constantly asking people to abandon what they believe in, in order to defend it.

Interviewer: But do you think it is necessary and acceptable to make your heroes so masochistic?
le Carré: In the sense that they enjoy being hurt?

Interviewer: And enjoy putting themselves in situations such as the spy who allowed himself to go into prison,[3] and I'm not at all sure he didn't rather enjoy himself in many ways while he was there.

---

3. Alec Leamas in *The Spy Who Came in From the Cold*.

le Carré: Yes, I think that's a splendid point. Perhaps there is this element in my book: that spies who work for big institutions, like the rest of us who work for big institutions, in fact need the discipline and pain of control; that they invite some kind of remote control of the smallest details of their lives; that in fact they are drawing some sense of union from the pain they get— like medieval monks, they really want to be flogged. Consider the case of Petrov—a Soviet intelligence agent who defected from a Soviet embassy in Canberra some years ago. It could be that Petrov, having accepted the smallest regulation of his life, having been told on what street corner to meet you or me, having been told at which garage to rent the car, what false number to give it, having communicated in secret—which gives an enormous cachet to communication—with his masters thousands and thousands of miles away, liked to feel on his back the blows of their discipline, and that when he defected this was the infuriated gesture of a child growing up, feeling its independence, and no longer wanting that control which its parents exerted.

Interviewer: Do you think your characters also have the death-wish?
le Carré: In a sense, yes; but that can come upon any of us who fill in that gap between the dream and the reality, the dream of power, the dream of marriage as a perfect institution, the dream of love as a magic carpet. Where we often fail—and this may be one of the qualities of real tragedy—is in the disproportion between the dream we had and the reality when we meet it. This is certainly something which I tried to illustrate in *The Looking-Glass War*. A group of people were led gradually to a point where they recognized the futility of their position in the Cold War, and from then on they act out left-over lives to kill, sustained by the image of the hot war, and yet acting out the hot war attitudes in the Cold War, until finally from their dream they select a man, train him, sustain him with images of the past, and then send him away into the cold reality of his mission, where he dies. He is their sacrificial victim. They have gone through the ritual which was inevitable because they borrowed an ethic from the past and applied it to the future, and this is one of the many qualities which we must discern, I'm sure, in practically every professional combatant.

Violent Image

Alan Watson / 1969

Reprinted from *Sunday Times* [London], 30 March 1969, pp. 55–57.
Copyright © *Sunday Times*. Reprinted by permission.

Tonight at 10.40 London Weekend Television shows John le Carré in on-the-spot conversation with Alan Watson at several formative places in his life. Here we publish an extract from their talk, beginning with one of le Carré's abiding preoccupations, personal and public violence.

Interviewer: Did you experience much violence yourself when you were a boy at school?
le Carré: Once, that I remember. The public school that I went to in those days was one which cultivated violence very much. I was once beaten. It was a ritual; we sat at prep. in the day room where the younger children were kept to work at their homework in the evenings, and the door was opened and the prefect came in and he then selected the boy who was going to be beaten in this silence. You were then walked out and down to a washroom and you held the taps of the basin and you put your head into the basin and you were then flogged by the prefect. And if I found the chap who did that to me now I'd fix him. That's violence, it made a horrible impression on me.

Interviewer: Was it much more violent because it was ritualistic?
le Carré: Yes. And because it belonged to the terror of discipline. It's outrageous to me that we should be trained as children to do that kind of thing to each other. There is another kind of violence which I experienced later as a school master, not at Eton. When I was a Duty Master one night and the prefect of the day came to me and said: "Excuse me, sir, X is trying to commit suicide," and I said "Oh, nonsense, where is he?" and as I rushed up the stairs I saw a little figure standing on the banister. By the time I got up, somebody had gathered him up and I said, acting casually, in the best British tradition, "Why do you want to do a thing like that?" and he said "I can't keep up, I can't make my bed quick enough, I can't eat breakfast quick enough, I can't clean my shoes, I can't prepare my homework." In other words, he couldn't

10

stand the pace. It's a form of brutality we're quite familiar with outside school, but it's the secondary kind of violence which these militarised institutions can do to somebody and they call it shaping you. I withstood it as a child, I'm not crying in my beer about it, but I find it monstrous.

Interviewer: What really makes you shy away from what some people would call discipline and others violence?
le Carré: I don't think other people *would* call it discipline; I'm absolutely in favour of discipline, I think that's part of the security a child needs. But violence repels me. I can't stand pain.

Interviewer: Have you ever been in a situation where you were able to discover for yourself that you were a physical coward?
le Carré: Oh, of course I have. One Christmas I went for a walk over some fields and I came across a pigeon that had been half eviscerated by a bird of prey and it needed killing and I couldn't kill it, and I turned my back on it and walked away. I call that cowardice. It's not true that joke about people who write about violence because they are innately violent and sublimate it in their work. I write about violence, I believe convincingly, because I frighten the skin off my own self. . . . What I try to do as a writer is to illustrate in my books the tensions which I feel myself. . . .

I feel surrounded by violence. It isn't a persecution mania, it's simply an awareness of the essential violence of people, the result of being inarticulate, the result of being overcrowded, of being pursued by noise.

Interviewer: You've been very successful; how rich have you actually become?
le Carré: Firstly, if I knew the answer, I don't think I'd reveal it. Secondly, I think, to me anyway, it's absolutely irrelevant. If you'd asked me the question three or four years ago, when it was all very new, then it would have worried me terribly, and I would have told you whatever lie I felt convenient at the time.

The truth is, you see, really that the equipment which I need for my life is simply a pen and a pad of paper, the rest of the equipment is peace and money has provided me with that. The capital outlay is small. I don't think that I'm awfully interested in happiness, that is to say the kind of commercial happiness like long holidays in the Bahamas. What I do know is this—that when the writing is going well I don't care about the money, and when it's going badly, the money's no consolation. . . .

I believe absolutely that I haven't written the book I would want to be buried with. Of course, I think all writers have that. They want first of all to be assessed on the body of their work and not on any one particular book, but they all, like the German Romantics, think they are looking for the blue flower and that the *Urbuch*, that is, the final definitive book about themselves or their work or how they live in society, is yet to come. And that's the only point of writing.

Interviewer: Meanwhile the machine and the industry goes on and the full exploitation of the books that you have written continues.
le Carré: Yes, that's right, and the bad ones get taken up just like the good ones.

Interviewer: How do you live with that?
le Carré: Well, to begin with, I don't define which are the good ones and which are the bad ones, that's the critics' job and far be it from me to do their job. In my own mind there is only one standard and that is that mysterious one of creative honesty—to what extent would I in that role really have said these things or felt these things? When you disintegrate your character and play each of the parts as you write the book, you animate each character so that it takes wing and you can relate to it because it has a bit of yourself in it and you have this God-like feeling of putting a fragment of your own identity into each one. You can tell which dialogue and situations are vamped, are hammed, where you are being an old entertainer and where you are breaking new ground. You are your best critic.

Interviewer: Do you think that your financial success has been largely dependent on Ian Fleming's James Bond books before you so that you were able to come in on the end of an espionage boom?
le Carré: Well, to hell with financial success, but the recognition and the kind of spur which the film and the book of the *Spy* made—all of that in a way I owe to Fleming. I think that I filled a gap. I think that Fleming did provide this curious visionary picture of a man who was given an identifiable enemy. Bond was always dignified by the enemies. He also, during the heat of the Cold War, failed to offer any serious comment about the Cold War. The result was that apart from the story of the *Spy*, which is what really sold it, and what fascinated people, there was I think a counter-market, if you can call it that, a counter-demand created by the saccharine picture of a perfect enemy, a

perfect hero, layable girls, the magic-carpet world of big expense accounts and crashable Ferraris. Well, I lived at the right time and wrote at the right moment and Fleming as I say created a hunger which I was able to satisfy, not by design but by chance, and if I'm to analyse in retrospect what happened to me *then*, then I doff my hat to Fleming, of course. I hadn't read Bond. It simply isn't possible to compose a best-seller which breaks new ground out of a sort of intellectual notion of what is required by a public you've never met. It's a one-time strike.

Interviewer: You owe a lot to Fleming, but you despise Bond?

le Carré: Oh yes, I despise Bond. I despise the short answer in the perfectly-made world. I believe that most of us live in doubt and that is what animated the people who read my book, they felt "Well gosh, this is organised chaos, there is no solution." I never knew a solution; you are constantly trying. I think that's what they recognise and then that put me in a corner where I seemed to be a guru, but I am really not a person of conviction. If I were I wouldn't write.

Interviewer: When you were a small boy you were largely brought up in the home of your grandfather, who was Mayor of Poole and a devout non-conformist. It was a household which was very sure of itself. . . .

le Carré: Yes, I think so. It certainly knew its own pattern of life and knew what it wanted from life, but it was also conscious of the erratic nature of human-kind and much more open to the notion of sin and suffering than one commonly supposes of doctrinally oriented people.

Interviewer: You were faced with this world which was not an unintelligent world, but a very certain world, a believing world, you were then faced with a lot of other very believing and certain worlds, Eton and the Foreign Office; this must have created a great confusion in you because you never really accepted any of them.

le Carré: Yes. That kind of background is exactly the background as I understand it that can produce a criminal mentality.

Interviewer: Is there then a meaningful relationship between the idea of the criminal and the idea of the author of your kind of book? The criminal rejects society, and he also creates his own society and his own order; so for that matter does the spy.

le Carré: I've often tried to draw this parallel between the writer and the spy. I don't think one should ever think of the writer as just a thief who steals all the components of his work and puts them together and offers them to the public; because you can steal as much as you like, but until you animate those components with some part of your own experience or compassion, until you dignify your own resentment, you haven't put together anything which people will read or relate to.

Interviewer: There are those that are going to say that because of this latest book of yours,[1] you have been disloyal to the class from which you come, to the group to which you belong. And in the *Spy* you certainly didn't belong anywhere. Do you belong?

le Carré: I've never felt I belong anywhere. I've been very lucky in that respect. I've had a very rich life up to now, I'm not talking about money, but I've come from a lot of places and none, and I've seen a lot of institutions and a lot of things. I've led a lot of lives in an odd way. I don't feel that I belong to any of them.

Interviewer: And have you been disloyal?

le Carré: That is just the point. The only disloyalty I'm concerned about is disloyalty to myself. ... Let me put it this way, one of the results of early success is confusion, a sense of indirection. And coupled with it is the obligation to live a romantic life. By romanticism I understand that one identifies one's private standards and adheres to them. This doesn't lead one to solid conclusions, and it doesn't restrain one with intellectual discipline. It leaves you on your own.

---

1. *A Small Town in Germany* (1968).

A Conversation with John le Carré

Robert G. Deindorfer / 1974

Reprinted from *Book-of-the-Month Club News*, June 1974, p. 4.

John le Carré, whose real name is David Cornwell, sat on the porch of his chalet on a shoulder of the Jungfrau high in the Swiss Alps. Galley proofs of his new novel littered a desk inside. Lighted by sunshine, skiers whooshed down a steep trail beyond a roll in the Alps. Cornwell took turns watching the skiers and answering phone calls from agents, publishers and lawyers calling from London, New York and Paris. At forty-two, Cornwell is wry, articulate, thoughtful. Fluent in three languages, he shuttles between homes in England and Switzerland with his wife and infant son. He did tours in two services frequently used as cover by British agents, has a bone-deep knowledge of the arcane craft of intelligence and doesn't mind talking about the game.

Interviewer: How did you come to write *Tinker, Tailor, Soldier, Spy*?
le Carré: Ever since *The Spy Who Came in From the Cold* I've been considering reversing the process by doing a book about a traitor inside our own service.

Interviewer: You successfully broke away from the form in your last novel, *The Naive and Sentimental Lover*. Why another spy thriller now?
le Carré: I never thought I was saying goodbye to spy stories by writing a different kind of book. I think the spy story is as capable of as much variation as the love story is. Spying and love are probably much closer as literary themes than one would suppose. After all, they're both to do with loyalty and they're both to do with the selection of life partners.

Interviewer: What made you use George Smiley again?
le Carré: I like him as a character. I find it attractive that he's so terribly expert in the conduct of his professional life and such a fumbler in the conduct of his private life. Professionally he's illusionless, and yet in love he's the victim of self-deception.

Interviewer: Then I expect you'll cast him in another book sometime? What about Karla, Smiley's Soviet counterpart?
le Carré: I can't believe that I would leave the battle between Smiley and Karla where it stands now. I can't leave them alone. I like to think in time it would reach some suitably tortuous solution.

Interviewer: Is British intelligence actually as bitter and political at the command level as the book suggests?
le Carré: My experience at every other sort of institution leads me to believe that the everyday intrigue we're all familiar with in the office, at home and in our other communities surely must find its way into an arena whose very existence is intrigue.

Interviewer: And what about the split-level morality. Your book paints the British service every bit as wicked, cynical and willing to write off human assets as the competitive Russian service.
le Carré: One tragedy of our present age is the fact that we have been forced into a position where we have to adopt the methods of our aggressors. There seems no way around this. But it does raise the question of how long we can go on defending ourselves by these methods and remain a society worth defending.

Interviewer: On the basis of your knowledge, how do you rate the major intelligence services in terms of efficiency?
le Carré: I honestly couldn't rate them. I do get impressions, of course. I have the impression, for example, that the Israelis are very good. I have the very definite impression that just as the Russians tremendously tend to overrate the American service, the Americans tremendously overrate the Russian service.

Interviewer: Intelligence does have a proper role, doesn't it?
le Carré: I think the standard charter for an intelligence service is to achieve by underhand means what a government is attempting to achieve by overt means. The trouble is that so few governments know exactly what they want to achieve. And so only rarely can the intelligence service determine and then pursue its own targets.

Interviewer: How do you concoct such subtle, elaborate, bewildering plots?
le Carré: I begin with a basic equation, two people with appetites operating in a single arena. Then I break the equation and turn it around and around

and around. I become absolutely obsessed by the possibilities of my plot. When I'm actually locked into one of these things I work all hours of the day and night, I have trouble sleeping, I eat very little, I keep a pen and pad beside my bed. It's like going on a cure. I enjoy it enormously. It's meat and drink.

Interviewer: What about your background?
le Carré: It's fairly conventional. I was privately educated in England and Switzerland. After my national military service in the intelligence corps I went up to Oxford. I taught French and German at Eton for two years, but I didn't really like teaching. I left to go into the foreign service. I finished my career as British consul in Hamburg. I left the foreign service when *The Spy Who Came in From the Cold* made me financially independent. And I've been writing ever since.

Interviewer: Is your view of the world as sour as it sounds?
le Carré: I think it's fairly bleak. We consistently create institutions which are much worse than the sum of our parts. And that depresses me very much indeed.

Schoolmaster Who Came in From the Cold

James Cameron / 1974

Reprinted from the *Daily Telegraph Magazine* [London], 28 June 1974, pp. 23–29. Copyright © *Daily Telegraph Magazine*.

The house hangs there on the edge of England; the escarpment falls over a hundred feet of rock and salty scrub to the sea. From here only the enormous ocean stirs and grumbles between us and America. It is the toe of the Cornish peninsula, Land's End indeed, where the island peters out into the Atlantic in a vast and stunning panorama.

You would think it a good place to forget conspiracy and the shadowy secrets of complicated treason. Yet in the days there we talked of little else.

This is the house of David Cornwell. The territorial association in the name is only chance, and perhaps not too many people know it anyway. Almost everyone, however, knows the name that inhabits David Cornwell professionally, and which is even more fortuitous. David Cornwell is John le Carré, a very different character altogether. David Cornwell is the former schoolmaster and Foreign Office man who momentarily concentrates on the pleasure he gets from his eyrie of a home; like me he has had so many that the last one is always best. John le Carré is the creator of a distinguished school of novels about espionage and the sombre loneliness of vulnerable traitors and spies who worry about their expense accounts. These two merge together in a tall and friendly brown-haired Englishman who is still a little baffled at having blundered on to one of the most phenomenal best-selling successes of the generation, yet who still very properly insists on taking himself seriously.

When David Cornwell wrote the famous *The Spy Who Came in From the Cold* he accomplished two things. He gave a new dimension to the spy-story in that he brought *style* to the making of essentially action novels, style and character and compassion and a rather haunting kind of verisimilitude. He also made a great deal of money.

Any writer to trade must read a le Carré story with envious regard for its technique, the elusive simplicity of its grey character-drawing against the

18

intricate craftsmanship of its plotting. It exists as a novel-of-manners outside its function as a thriller. It follows that Cornwell-le Carré would have been a writer even without his identification with the creepier sub-world of international intelligence.

He produced two moderate books, *Call for the Dead* in 1961 and *A Murder of Quality* in 1962, before he came upon his prime invention, the bitter fall-guy Alec Leamas, the spy who came in from the cold, and hit the jackpot with a more resounding bang than any British novelist since the war. There were twelve impressions in six months. The sales must now approach twenty million. Then came *The Looking-Glass War*, and bingo again: £145,000 for the paperback rights alone. Say a le Carré book is now worth about half-a-million sterling. That makes David Cornwell very rich indeed. It is a troublesome subject for conversation, unbecoming to a morning of sparkling spacious beauty on a Cornish clifftop. It could of course equally have been a Schloss or a chateau or a chalet or a Cayman cabana; the money nowadays would run to any of them, or indeed probably all. It is however most existentially English, as is David Cornwell, however many tentative tries he has had to be otherwise.

Here are three farm workers' cottages welded most beautifully together, thick granite walls with windows like embrasures to defend the house against the terrible winter winds. When the storms come they tear at the roof, and the waves a hundred feet below send up a stinging spray. Tiny plants shrivel in desperation behind little barricades; in the end the salt gets them.

On a day of perfection like this, however, the house is poised against the basking horizon of a tranquil pewter-coloured sea. It is a long way from the Berlin Wall, or the Soho alleys where the Circus[1] has its being in the le Carré processes, or the raincoated solitude of the superannuated spy. This is Cornwell's Cornwall, not the neurotic insecurity of John le Carré's unholy underworld.

In the broadest terms, why has John le Carré's secret-service-dirty-tricks *oeuvre* gone down with the public so extraordinarily well?

"Very few people aren't interested in deceit—intelligence work, espionage. It's the contemporary arena of the Cold War. People have always been fascinated in the anatomy of betrayal. Judas is a very memorable character.

1. The headquarters of the British secret service in le Carré's novels is located at Cambridge Circus, London.

Most people are to some degree absorbed by the modern machinery of conspiracy. If you take the conventional melodrama out of it the thing becomes com-
prehensible in human terms. Alec Leamas is a very commonplace chap with
banal inadequacies precipitated into a situation of fantasy and conditioned to
respond in a special way. So is George Smiley,[2] in a different way—he only had
a bit part in *The Spy*, but he's the main thing in *Tinker, Tailor, Soldier, Spy*.

"The fact is they belong to the wrong time. There's a sense that their thing
is running down. Say what you like, there's a nostalgia for the Cold War. (In
Looking-Glass War there's a nostalgia for the hot war.) You have to get the
texture and the mood of that. After every war there's a period of ruefulness.
Look at all these television series on the first and second wars; it's a reversion
to the exciting past because of the dismal present.

"They're trying to dismantle the Dulles[3] era, which was the Cold War heyday. I was with my sons in Berlin a little while ago and toured that bloody
Wall, and East Berlin; we're now all supposed to call it the DDR. That's all
right. But one forgets that it wasn't long ago that German emigré people,
refugees, went in actual fear of their lives, the place was so insecure. It's still
there for operators like my middle-aged George Smiley; no wonder he's in a
state of total ideological disorientation. They needed the obvious tensions . . .

"As soon as the Russians took the heat off Europe it began to disintegrate.
Look at the incoherence now. Take us: look at our elements of dissent. Look
at something like *Private Eye*:[4] it sniggers about pooves and sex like a Fifth
Form dirty joke. It's symptomatic of Englishness that we no longer know
what to laugh at or what to dissent from."

Such considerations seem somewhat remote here. The room is big and
simple and nice; a gentle aromatic smog from burning logs. On the shelves a
number of books; not as many as expected. "The library got mixed up changing homes." Not mixed up here, though: rows of collected works—forty-eight
volumes of Balzac in the Caxton edition, Hardy, Wodehouse, Proust,
Dickens, Greene, Shaw, Maupassant, neat as guards of honour.

"I don't read much new fiction. No modern spy stories; no, I haven't read
any Len Deighton. I like some of the Americans—Updike, Bellow. And
Sybille Bedford.[5] I find you don't read much if you write."

2. The key character in the early le Carré novels.
3. Allen Dulles was the Director of the Central Intelligence Agency (CIA) from 1953 to 1961.
4. British satirical magazine.
5. British social novelist (1911–).

To return to our author. David John Moore Cornwell was born in Poole
forty-three years ago. His grandfather was a builder who became Mayor of
Poole, a vigorous nonconformist lay-preacher, no Sunday newspapers, and
plenty of prayer. He lived there awhile. His father was a well-to-do business
man of sporting tastes, who among other things owned racehorses and stood
as a Liberal candidate.[6] David Cornwell sees him rarely now. The boy was
sent to Sherborne, a public school of somewhat relentless piety; when they
told him life was a simple conflict between God and Mammon, he quietly
walked out, and went to study German literature at the University of Bern,
where he was deeply lonely for nine months.

It was a *mouvementé* life. He served in the Army in Austria. He went to
Lincoln College, Oxford, and took a first in modern languages and got married for the first time. When someone offered him a job as an assistant master at Eton he grabbed it for the security; it paid £650 a year, with £90
deducted for rents. That was in 1956 and 1957. He found Eton intolerably
insulating, left the job for an essay at freelance illustrating, answered an
advertisement for late entrants to the Foreign Office and joined the
Diplomatic Service. He served two and a half years as Second Secretary at the
Embassy in Bonn (this experience provided the inspiration for *A Small Town
in Germany*). He was political consul in Hamburg when *The Spy Who Came
in From the Cold* hit the big bonanza and released David Cornwell into the
world of letters in the form of John le Carré.

All this David Cornwell describes with a most rare and unexpected comedian's gift; he is the most talented of raconteurs in a studied variety of professional accents—an earnest Russian *kulturnik*, an American radio interviewer,
a barmy British Ambassador in Asia, a profoundly convincing Harold
Macmillan.[7] The David Cornwell Show of protean impersonation is a special
bonus.

His wife Jane, whom he married in 1971, is cooking an omelette. Their
small blond son Nicholas is thudding about with the total assurance of
fifteen months, a beloved child. From the other marriage there is Simon at
seventeen and Stephen at fourteen, both at Westminster, and Timo at prep
school. There is also an animated doormat of a sheepdog called Smith, whose

6. See the 9 October 1977 *Washington Post* interview for Cornwell's discussion of his father's
criminal activities.
7. British Prime Minister (1957–1963).

reputation for a razor-sharp intelligence is belied by a dotty and indiscriminate affection for strangers. It is a very happy place.

One had to get the question over fairly soon—that is: what does it mean to
a writer, normally a pretty submerged man, suddenly to become quite star-
tling rich—that is to say, when through your own work money becomes virtually limitless?

"It was confusing for a while. I wrote the books for money, but not for
that much money. I admit I don't particularly like talking about it. Not
because I'm modest or evasive; but now I've got all I can use there's nothing
much to say. What would you say?"

I said I would ask myself seriously why I came back and deliberately
exposed myself to giving the tax-man most of what I had made, when I was
rich enough to do otherwise.

"I tried the otherwise. It was very nice. The Greek islands, Paris, America,
Vienna, Switzerland. Full of advantages. Then I weighed it up and decided I
wanted to live in England. I like English values, I want my children to have
English friends. It suits us here."

The price was of course very high. As a British resident he has to pay a
truly gruesome mountain of tax. Self-employed writers are all punitively
taxed anyway; David Cornwell's bill is more like a Budget.

"But wouldn't it be the most asinine thing in the world if success *limited*
your freedom? I don't honestly see why having a lot of money should prevent
me living where I want to. I want to have my home here, and I'm readily paying the bill for it. I'm a writer, not a financier. What is important is that I
don't get trapped in the best-seller machine. That's all there is to it, techni-
cally. I work better here. Money is great, but let's say: if the writing is going
well you don't want it, and if it's going badly it's no consolation."

I suggested that in between times it must be rather helpful. If I had struck
oil in a book to the tune of half-a-million or so I would surely never write
another word, except on cheques. I would put John le Carré out to grass and
dive back into David Cornwell like a shot.

"I don't know. Before I gave up my job the thing that governed my writing
was simply shortage of time, which was a damned nuisance; I wrote on
trains, in lunch-hours. I suppose in a way I was fortunate in having boring
jobs. Now I'm lucky enough to have everything anyone could want for good
working conditions, except the necessary anxieties. If you haven't got real
tensions you've got to invent them. . . . I wrote *The Spy* in five months. The
others took about three years.

"I heard once that Picasso, who was damned rich . . . after his mistress had written a book, he got a telegram asking him to join an appeal for the release of Russian writers, and he replied: 'They write better in prison.' It was terribly brutal, but it was probably artistically right."

I asked about the le Carré preoccupation with the German theme; sometimes its atmospheric compulsion seems almost obsessive. Myself having mostly uneasy and ragged memories of the postwar days, of the Berlin Blockade, of a country forever talking behind its hands. What were the origins of his love-hate relationship?

"It's a fairly big part of me. I studied in a German-speaking University, I read German at Oxford, I taught the language at Eton, I served some years in the Foreign Service in Germany. I somehow appreciated the tension. They are industrious and clever and naive; they grope intuitively to authoritarian absolutes. I suppose I made the Germans a reflection of my own potential. I made Germany my Wild West—the heroes and villains are clearly definable by recent history; this is helpful.

"The truth is of this kind of fiction that it must proceed from the cliché, if only to reduce it *to* cliché. No, perhaps 'assumption' is a better word. In fact the novel is really a middle-class sport; it rests on certain middle-class assumptions: that treason goes against the grain, in a way like adultery. My framework must somehow run counter to this. In *Looking-Glass War*, for instance, the characters didn't fulfil the heroic role their origins required; that is the point. The novel hasn't progressed much since Balzac.

"In *A Small Town in Germany* I had this British diplomat, an idealistic sort of figure who wants to expose the new Hitler-ethic, and is frustrated not by *them* but by *us*. The question is: does the man of decent and solid principles stand any chance of being effective in this sort of world? Honestly I don't know; maybe we have handed over to the hypocrites and compromisers."

We bought up what, after the matter of making money, seems to be required journalistic discussion with Cornwell-le Carré: how much of the Intelligence background and detail derives from personal experience. After all, he served in a sensitive Embassy and cannot have failed to be touched by the subterranean goings-on that inform almost all German activity. The spy-novels have this wholly persuasive air of authenticity, even to reducing everything to the deliberately prosaic. In a word, was he at one time on the game himself?

"Look at it like this: if you or I write a novel about a brothel-keeper, people wouldn't at once assume that we'd *been* brothel-keepers. At least I imagine not. I know a bit about the complex characters that operate in my sort of story. The narrative derives from those characters and the tensions they generate within themselves. The story of *The Spy* was really a story of loneliness; it was in a Cold War context which gave it the edge."

There were stories that the Foreign Office had been displeased at the horrid accuracy of the Intelligence background, which is why he left the Service.

"Not a bit. In fact there was a sort of an attempt to keep me on. The pseudonym? It was considered proper that Foreign Service officials should not publish under their real names. I got John le Carré from a London shopfront I once passed on a bus. If you want to see any mystery in it, that's all right.

"I clear the names of the fictional agents through the Office, just in case I should accidentally blunder on a real name. I did once, and they got me to change it."

David Cornwell does his writing in the mornings; like all stylists he does not work on a typewriter. He says he overwrites enormously—something like half-a-million words come down to a booklength of about 90,000 through a long sequence of revised drafts. ("Someone said you get talent in the first draft, art in the other ones.") He needs a lot of solitude. A book is a very private trip; while it is happening he will not discuss it at all with anyone.

"When it's done I try to get a new one under way as soon as I can, to overtake the worries and reservations everyone has about a book when it's finished." Bad notices upset him; he finds some of them perverse and unfair; there is a tendency with critics to be bitchy about assured successes. Jane Cornwell now insulates him from anything really wounding.

One aspect of the work interested me, though I should not have found it surprising: he does *photographic* research. The trademark of a le Carré narrative, apart from the bleak and generally joyless character of the preoccupied *demi-monde* that sidles through it, is the vivid sense of environment, of actuality in location: an area of activity is defined precisely. le Carré's mysterious Circus is based in Cambridge Circus at the New Compton Street corner—and there are photographs of the actual building, from several angles, even the particular office rooms identified. It is as though David Cornwell the impresario has to reassure John le Carré the executant that he must not stray from the recognisable commonplace setting into the exotic, just as his agents and conspirators must not stray into lyricism from the recognisable characters of commonplace and unhappy men.

I asked about the films: had they measured up to his concept of the book, how personally involved had he been?

"I sometimes wish producers would use the European technique and employ unknown actors for these parts; it would give the script a better chance than casting stars, but it's too much to ask. I don't know much about film-writing. I spent a year with Jack Clayton on *The Looking-Glass War*, and in the end we didn't do it. Same with Karel Reisz on *The Naive and Sentimental Lover*. We've got different values. In their field they're too good to accept my work, and in mine I'm too good to accept theirs. Now I sell to the best bidder and forget about it."

The new novel, *Tinker, Tailor, Soldier, Spy*, is very markedly in direct line of descent from *The Spy Who Came in From the Cold*, more so in my view than from the others, and probably the best one yet. (There is a riotously engaging new character in Connie Sachs.) I should say it asks rather a lot from its readers in concentration or familiarity with the old obliquities and allusive codewords: "witchcraft," "Lamplighters," "Listeners," "Scalphunters," "Babysitters," everything naturally meaning otherwise than what it seems to mean.

"I'm just a little concerned about the structuring of the book; it's quite complex. But the resolution at the end says a lot of the things I feel about defection, basic treachery, and so on."

Kim Philby,[8] for instance. He was interested to know I had had an acquaintanceship with him in Beirut.

"Most absorbing fellow. . . . I had a difference of opinion with Graham Greene over Philby; we take different views. I'm obliged to say that I feel Philby was essentially dead wrong all the way through and all the time. I don't think the ideology was especially important to him, and certainly the money wasn't. But his consistent objective was to get rid of the values and conditions I hold to be all right, and I don't go along with it."

David Cornwell recently got back from a longish trip through South East Asia, which greatly touched his imagination; I would imagine it is certain that the next le Carré will move east for the first time.

"Yes, I saw Vietnam. And yes, I hate the Americans for what happened in Vietnam. It's a marvellously eloquent metaphor for what's happening to the rest of the world."

8. (1912–1988); British traitor who defected to the Soviet Union in 1963.

He went to the desk and got out a cloth tunic-patch which read: "Kill a Commie for Christ."

"That's the sickest thing I know. Even if it's satire it's just as sick. As someone said: a nation goes from barbarism to decadence in 150 years."

"Without an intervening period of civilisation."

"Exactly."

So I would suppose that David Cornwell has already got John le Carré to work on South East Asia.

"I don't think Vietnam; Graham Greene defined that for all time in *The Quiet American*; it stands up brilliantly still."

The Cornish sea sighed on the rocks far below. Smith, the mobile muff, made indications suggesting the need for a breath of air.

"I don't know if you noticed, there's one thing the books have in common. They almost all begin and end at odd hours of the night. That's to say—it all never began and it never finished. After the resolution comes the resumption. Just like every revolution leaves a pre-revolutionary condition. The whole thing is a continuum. It's open-ended."

"And the books will go on."

"Of course."

John le Carré: The Writer Who Came in From the Cold

Michael Dean / 1974

Reprinted from *The Listener*, 92 (5 September 1974), pp. 306–7. Copyright ©
The Listener. From an interview on BBC 2. Reprinted by permission.

Interviewer: *The Spy Who Came in From the Cold* was your first big success, but much further back, what was the first story you remember writing?
le Carré: I wrote at prep school. I had a great fondness for animals; children do, for a while, and I wrote a short story, quite a long short story for a boy, about an old heroic racehorse who was ridden to victory by an unscrupulous jockey who had loaded his whip with buckshot, and I thought this really was the most moving tragedy I had ever read, let alone written. I persuaded the headmaster's secretary to type it out for me and she, in turn, was discovered doing this by the headmaster who was tremendously angry and brought the stuff back to me, untyped, and said that if I wanted to write trash I should get it typed out in my own way and not use his resources. I don't think that would happen these days, but a little repression doesn't do us any harm. There is a terrible moment in the memoirs of Picasso's mistress where he receives a telegram inviting him to associate himself with a protest against the imprisonment of Russian writers and he replies, as he throws away the telegram: "They write better in prison." I think that was the principle by which I began writing at prep school.

Interviewer: In *Tinker, Tailor, Soldier, Spy* there is an almost painfully vivid picture of a run-down prep school: how important was the experience of prep school in your development?
le Carré: Very important, in a sense. I had no consistent family life and therefore, as a child, I was already very concerned with the institutions which were outside my family. We lived an itinerant life when I was a child and I went from school to school and developed a very wary eye for each new place that I was attached to. I also went to a succession of holiday schools and I developed the habit, like a soldier on the move, of picking out the best bed in the dormitory, fixing an eye on the most susceptible lady members of the staff,

27

getting to know the cook; a technique of survival inside what I tended to regard as an atavistic community.

Interviewer: The lonely outsider who occurs in your fiction, the failed boy, is he, in any way, a part of your own childhood?
le Carré: I think that in a way he is. I really don't believe that when one writes about a character it is possible to distance him too much from one's own feelings and experience. Later, when I was a schoolmaster, I taught at a prep school, which was not run-down or bad like the one I described in my new book, and there was a little boy who was terribly good at one subject. As far as I remember it was arithmetic. One night, about my first night as duty master, I was sitting before a great Victorian fireplace rather nervously reading the *Spectator*, waiting for the boys to be got to bed so that I could go round and say goodnight and tuck them down, when the prefect of the day came in and said: "Please, Sir, X is trying to commit suicide." I remember running up the great Victorian stair-well and seeing this little fat boy with spectacles poised on the bannisters and he certainly could have done himself to death as he fell down. By the time I got up to the top, another boy had seized him round the tummy and pulled him off the bannisters. He was quite white and had nothing very much to say, and when I got him alone and we talked it over, he said: "Well, you see, I'm just not very good at making my bed and I'm not very good at arranging my day, and I never have the right books and I don't think I'm fit for this place." I'm sure that particular experience played a part in describing exactly the fears that haunted the little boy in the book, a terrible feeling of administrative inadequacy.

Interviewer: Why did you become a teacher?
le Carré: I think in the first place because the job was there. I had two spells of teaching; the first was as a prep schoolmaster before I took my degree. I went down from Oxford for a year and taught at a prep school, Evelyn Waugh-style, and just as I was finishing at Oxford, it became news that Eton wanted someone to teach modern languages. Somebody sidled up and offered me the job, which so often happens in that establishment world.

In some ways, those who knock the upper classes have no idea how awful they are. Eton, at its worst, is unbelievably frightful. It is intolerant, chauvinistic, bigoted, ignorant. At its best, it is enlightened, adaptable, fluent and curiously democratic.

Interviewer: Was it a natural progression from Eton to diplomacy?

le Carré: Yes, in a way. Eton gave me familiarity with crime, as well as an instinct for hypocrisy and both of them, in different ways, are not absolutely unknown in diplomacy. Again, it was an institutional pull. I am quite unashamed about my interest in English institutions, and I've always been slightly moralistic and puritanical about making contributions, doing something useful. If this is what you feel, then you put your effort where your mouth is, but it didn't work for me, really, because I was doing the wrong job. I should have been writing; I didn't know that at the time.

Interviewer: When did you know?

le Carré: I knew as I went on conforming. I knew by the time I left Eton that I couldn't remain inside such a place and go on with repetitive teaching and turning over the harvest of boys every three or four years. I knew, equally, after a short while in the Foreign Service, that I could not accept these forms of conformity. I just sneaked off and wrote in my spare time as a way of asserting my freedom, or trying to define my own identity. I was commuting then from Great Missenden; the line wasn't electrified, and I started writing my first book in little notebooks on the train. I thought the first book was quite good. The second book was about a school and that, I think, I wrote in Bonn, just after my first posting, and then, with the Berlin Wall, I began writing *The Spy Who Came in From the Cold*, and wrote it very quickly. But all of those first three books I wrote in the early mornings and during the transportation between work and home, so I knew by the time I had finished writing *The Spy Who Came in From the Cold* that I had the makings of some sort of literary or artistic strength. What makes me go on working, what makes me go on writing, is the hope that one day I'll do something I'm really proud of.

Interviewer: It was said, at the time, by some, that you were writing a consciously anti-Bond spy-thriller.

le Carré: That was nonsense. I'm not nearly clever enough to have done that at the time, and I wrote about the things that I knew of, the tensions in Berlin which I witnessed: institutional behaviour, British nostalgia for power, perhaps, and I imported from my experience of the Foreign Service a great deal of the way paper is moved around and the dinginess of decisions, sometimes. It doesn't necessarily mean they are smaller decisions, but they are taken in small rooms. The material available to me was entirely different from the material available to Fleming. Fleming had a glamorous brother who came from a wealthy family. A lot of flip things were said about *The Spy* to make him anti-Bond, and a number of basic ingredients in the story were over-looked. It is a very romantic story: two people fall in love and one has to betray the other and both of them, in a sense, perish in a mental institution; both of them, in the same breath, make a statement in favour of humanity. Basically, what was there was a romantic story, and, dare I say it myself, a very well-told one, and that is what people want to read.

Interviewer: Did the success of *Spy* force you to repeat the form or stick with the thriller genre?
le Carré: Yes. I tend to believe that it is the kind of writing I do best. I do not really think of myself as writing essentially spy stories, but it is a very danger-ous area, because I hate making grand pretensions for my books.

Interviewer: I have noticed that you have a remarkably accurate ear. How good is your eye?
le Carré: In the first instance, I have absolutely no geographical sense. I can never work out which way the house faces. If I am in London, or anywhere, I can never find my way from one place to another. I think I have an eye for visual detail, which stands me in good stead for making characters have little mannerisms, habits of dressing, twitches, particular features that seem expressive, grimaces. I think it is true that, sometimes, in compiling a charac-ter, one pinches this mannerism, that habit of speech, this form of dress and puts them together into a sort of package. It is a bit like a spy stealing from a community of which he is a part, and, adding to that, the fire of one's own imagination. The way people walk characterises the person for you, too. For instance, that angular, bouncy walk Treasury civil servants do seem to have, which is very good in *Monty Python*, that strange way of springing on the toe and moving forward onto the other leg.

Interviewer: Why do you find it necessary then to reinforce this very good memory you have got for physical detail with your own photography?
le Carré: I photographed, for instance, all the locations in *Tinker, Tailor, Soldier, Spy*. I blew up the photographs, partly to give me documentary help. Cambridge Circus, where I set the Secret Service headquarters, has this mar-vellous red-brick building with a bank down below, and the last time I went

to look at it, to work out a scene which was being played round there, I saw, to my horror, the building had been pulled down. I thought, well, I must keep it, even if they can't, so I photographed all of that. The face of London changes so quickly, I want to use all these buildings for future books on the Secret Service; so I've frozen them and put them in the bank.

Interviewer: If pressed, would you say you were a novelist, or what?
le Carré: I would just say writer, I think. One has enough problems without doing the critic's job. There is this endless debate about the difference between a thriller and a novel, and it really is a very feeble one. There are, of course, books which are written in such a mechanical way that you impose upon the characters forms of behaviour. You have to get the parson into the wood-house at 2 a.m. in order to kill the duchess. Now that is a book where the plot is imposed upon the characters, and the characters hang around in the country house, until somebody screams upstairs and everybody clicks into life. There is the other kind of book where you take one character, you take another character and you put them into collision, and the collision arrives because they have different appetites, and you begin to get the essence of drama. The cat sat on the mat is not a story; the cat sat on the dog's mat is the beginning of an exciting story, and out of that collision, perhaps, there comes a sense of retribution. Now you may call that God, or you may call it the presence of fatalistic forces in society, or you may call it man's inhumanity to man. But, in the immortal words of P. G. Wodehouse, what it boils down to is that if your character does something wrong, sooner or later if he walks down a dark street, fate will slip out with a stuffed eel-skin and get him.

Interviewer: It strikes me that there are a number of inconsistencies, or contradictions about your existence. Here you are living on the butt-end of Cornwall, and that window leads all the way to America. You are an Englishman who, for tax reasons, I suppose, ought to be living in the South of France, or Switzerland, writing for an audience which is overwhelmingly American.
le Carré: First of all, of course, I rely on an English life for my books. I wrote one book, *The Looking-Glass War*, on the island of Crete, and I had the greatest difficulty to remember even how the English talk to one another. It was awfully hard, for my material is here, and my friends are here, but it is true that when I publish a book, the English reaction, apart from personal pride

and so on, is absolutely secondary to the American reaction, the German and even the French. The French market is probably more important to me financially than the English one. One of the great advantages of writing in English, and being a successful writer is that you have, immediately, the Anglo-Saxon market at your disposal. If *The Spy Who Came in From the Cold* had been written in Icelandic, I don't know whether it would ever have been a best-seller in America.

Interviewer: Could you ever contemplate leaving this country for good?
le Carré: If I did, I think I would go to Paris, and perhaps change the English countryside for the urban sophistication of Paris. Paris, as a city, is the place I like best, but I've done a lot of living abroad. I have been in exile for years on end, the enforced exile of being a foreign servant, the elected exile of going to Crete for a year and writing a book there. I was in Vienna for six months, a long time in the States messing around. I've done enough of that for the time being. At the moment my strong wish is to remain here.

Interviewer: You have written better than any other writer about the loneliness of the spy. In a sense, it is a loneliness, if not a morality, you share. The loneliness of the writer, I suppose, is something you are stuck with. Are you a lonely person?
le Carré: I think so, yes. I am often uncomfortable in company, and yet I am insufficient in myself. I am easily bored, and I think that turns me very much to amusing myself by writing at the entertainment level. I have a very low threshold of boredom, if that's the right expression. You have to be a bit of an Ancient Mariner, and I have to be that to myself, to keep myself in my chair while I'm working.

The Things a Spy Can Do:
John le Carré Talking

Melvyn Bragg / 1976

Reprinted from *The Listener*, 22 January 1976, p. 90. Copyright © *The Listener*. *Read All About It* (BBC 1). Reprinted by permission.

Interviewer: One of the striking things about the language in the book [*Tinker, Tailor, Soldier, Spy*] is the words which you use as technical terms—words like "lamplighters," "scalphunters," "mothers." What does "lamplighters" mean?

le Carré: Lamplighters were the courier service which serviced agents abroad and stepped into areas where the local Secret Service resident couldn't handle the job for himself.

Interviewer: And "scalphunters"?

le Carré: A scalphunter was a strong-arm man who did the really hard-nose, mail-fist operation.

Interviewer: What about the "mothers"?

le Carré: The mothers were senior white-haired ladies who worked for the head of the Secret Service and kept his secrets.

Interviewer: Were they also the "babysitters"?

le Carré: No, the babysitters were the bodyguards who covered the clandestine meetings.

Interviewer: Could you tell us what a "honey trap" was?

le Carré: A honey trap was where you put a girl in a chap's way. It's a sexual enticement operation.

Interviewer: And are these words real words, or did you invent them?

le Carre: All of those, I think, are made up, although I'm pleased to see that one or two have gone into the language. I've used some authentic words where I've been able to discover them, but I prefer my own, really. A "mole" is, I think, a genuine KGB term for somebody who burrows into the fabric of a bourgeois society and undermines it from within—somebody of the Philby sort who is recruited at a very tender age. The CIA call them "sleepers," I think. They're people about whom, at a certain time, you guess the pattern of their ideological development, if you're a talent-spotter working for the Russian Secret Service, and you winkle them into a corner, and say: "We appreciate your feelings about this, but just keep very quiet—sooner or later we will need you and when we do we will tell you."

Interviewer: Did you make a point of clearing all the agents' names with the Foreign Office to make sure you don't get anybody into trouble?
le Carré: Well, it's not quite as dramatic as that. I used to work for the Foreign Service, and as a sort of doffing of the cap, I still submit my books, which one, in theory, is supposed to do, and they still clear them.
It is a nightmare I have that, one of these days, I will invent a genuine operational situation and upset something terrible.

Interviewer: I suppose that I'm forced to ask the question that everybody wants to ask—I mean, were you, in fact, a spy?
le Carré: In the army, for my National Service, about 108 years ago, I worked with an extremely down-at-heel interrogation unit where we were trying to coax people across the Czechoslovak border and clean them of information, de-brief them. And, of course, you can't be in the Foreign Service for as long as I was without feeling the wind of those people. But I wish I could some-how shake off that image. If you write a story about street girls in London, you aren't immediately accused of running a brothel. But if you write a spy story, the more credible, the more authentic, the more plausible it is, the less credit you get for an active imagination. I'd much rather have plausibility than authenticity—that is, after all, the writer's trade.

Interviewer: Oddly enough, although you yourself have described *Tinker, Tailor, Soldier, Spy* as a spy novel—and it is a marvelous spy story—one of the things which grabbed me very much about it was how much it enables you to talk about politics.
le Carré: Yes, I enjoy that very much, and I think the scope of the spy story has yet to be discovered for that purpose. You see, an Intelligence operative is supposed to distinguish himself from the ordinary bureaucrat because he

acts. He does things where others talk. You know, you have the smoke-filled boardroom, and the prime minister sitting there, and everybody grinding his own axe; he walks away into a small room, and there are two guys in grey flannel suits, and they say: "Shall we just cut his throat for you?" So they're the people who actually combine thought with deeds. To that extent, they are the infantry of our ideology.

At the moment, when we have no ideology, and our politics are in a complete shambles, I find it a convenient microcosm, to shuffle around in a secret world and make that expressive of the overt world.

Interviewer: And because the hero of your book, Smiley, is perhaps the most contemporary hero that one can think of, his ambiguities of feeling about everything, including politics, are what sustain the central idea of the book.
le Carré: Yes, and it's that that I love best about him and about the book. In fact, he reminds me of a character in an earlier book of mine who said: "You know, my job is to lie for the good of my country, but my problem is I don't know what the truth is."

Interviewer: Do you think that Smiley's worries about his ideological position are worries which are around people who do that sort of operation, or are they worries that you fictionalise?
le Carré: I think that, to some extent, they're around in people who do that kind of operation—I think they're very much around in thinking executives. There are a lot of people who believe that their own doubts are subordinate to the national need, and where they can identify the national need they very honourably try to achieve it.

It's a rather religious commitment—doubt, in a sense, is anti-ecclesiastic. I do believe those doubts are very much found, insofar as the book achieved a popular resonance when it first came out, particularly in the States. I think it did exactly catch a mood where values are dissolving so fast that we just want to stop the film running and look at one frame. Smiley says himself that there is a point in every man's life when he decides whether he will stop and say: "This is my generation. This is how I'm going to behave." But attitudes and events are turning over so fast that you aren't allowed to do that any more. Ever since the hot war turned into the Cold War and the Cold War turned into détente, we've gone through a succession of lunatic ideological reversals: people who were bombing Berlin in 1945 were running the airlift in 1948, and it's gone back and forth ever since. So Smiley is a committed doubter, and to that extent, I think, an extremely contemporary figure.

Interviewer: But political doubt is a metaphor of the whole book because every relationship is necessarily insincere.
le Carré: It's necessarily insincere. Every relationship, I think, is fraught with a nerve-wracking tension. That, to be truthful, is how I see life.

Interviewer: In short, nobody can trust anybody else?
le Carré: In short, we have to be enormously cautious with our commitments—yes. I think all of us live partly in a clandestine situation. In relation to our bosses, our families, our wives, our children, we frequently affect attitudes to which we subscribe perhaps intellectually, but not emotionally. We hardly know ourselves—nine-tenths of ourselves are below the level of the water.

One of the greatest realities is sex, but we almost never succeed in betraying our sexuality to one another fully. So the figure of the spy does seem to me to be almost infinitely capable of exploitation for purposes of articulating all sorts of submerged things in our society.

Interviewer: The book is so complicated in its plotting, by contemporary standards, that it compares with the intricate plotting of Dickens's novels. Do you actually sit down and map out this complicated series of events?
le Carré: Well, I do periodically, but I don't stick to the map. Occasionally, I just get completely lost. I seem to begin with one character, and then I begin setting others around him, and bring them into collision, and out of that I begin to get a plot. After thirty or forty pages, I begin to see the way it's going, and I'll make notes to myself. Then, probably, I'll take anything up to six months writing the first chapter; but then it's all banking up behind, and I begin to see the structure.

Interviewer: You don't sit down and say: "It must happen this way."
le Carré: No, I can't do it. I find the moment that I put down a real matrix, I press myself in irons. I can't do it. With *The Spy Who Came in From the Cold*, I reversed the plot quite arbitrarily, and right at the end of the book turned the whole thing inside out. Quite often, you have that feeling of revelation: how ridiculous, I've been straining to make this character sympathetic when actually he is an identifiable beast.

Interviewer: Do you enjoy the minor characters? The book is full of small parts.

le Carré: I love those small parts. If you're developing one or two characters in a book, you've really got to leave the others rather carelessly sketched in, otherwise they get out of scale. Mine are always getting out of scale. But I've got over that now by using them as industrial waste for the next book or the book after that. I promise them a treat in the next book, if they'll just keep quiet now.

A Visit with the Author

Elizabeth Easton / 1977

Reprinted from *Book-of-the-Month Club News*, Special Fall Edition 1974, p. 4.

I met David Cornwell in London, where he lives when he is not at home in the west of England close to Land's End in Cornwall. He says he spends about half his time in the city, the other half in the country working as the writer John le Carré.

Interviewer: What started you as a writer?
le Carré: Being broke, mainly—and being bored. I've always been very easily bored, and I come from a family which is not in the least bookish. I never read much as a child, and I'm still a very lazy reader now.

Interviewer: Weren't you a teacher?
le Carré: Yes, I was. I've overcome it. But I had been doing rather bad, commercial drawing—book covers and things like that—in my spare time while I was a schoolmaster, and then when I took the late entry exam to the British Foreign Service I found myself tremendously bored working at the Foreign Office in London. I was a commuter then, living down in Great Missenden. Instead of reading newspapers I began writing my first novel in little notebooks on the train.

Interviewer: You and Trollope.
le Carré: (Laughing) That's right. And then I started making a little bit of money out of it. I also found it obsessive. I found while sitting at my desk that I thought of very little else apart from my book and I quickly knew that I was giving to writing the best part of my life, that the ordinary routine that I was living was really just there to support it. So I told my accountant—I think with my third book, which was *The Spy Who Came in From the Cold*—that if ever I was worth £20,000 would he send me a cable? In those days it seemed enough to resign from the Foreign Office. He sent me a cable and I resigned.

38

Interviewer: You've set a style in the espionage novel that a lot of people have imitated. Which writers influenced you?

le Carré: Greene, of course. Conrad I love, and then I like the sort of solid Victorian storytellers very much. I like Balzac particularly, Balzac who made a continuing saga out of his characters, out of the creatures of his imagination. I notice that Greene in his autobiography says what I suspect to have been true of Balzac as well: that really the creatures of his imagination are much more real than the people he meets.

Interviewer: This is true of you?

le Carré: I think so, yes. I think it's becoming true in a way.

Interviewer: What's given you the most pleasure in the last year?

le Carré: Ah, writing. Without the smallest doubt.

Interviewer: Writing, not being published?

le Carré: Oh yes. I dislike being published very much. I like to get the books done. I mean if I painted the picture hanging on the wall I know that I would be wanting to jump up and alter this leaf or that one until the day of my death. But once you publish and it's printed, that's it. I think at the moment I'm just very happy about my professional situation, not only because people are paying me lots of money which secures my future and that kind of thing, but I feel, particularly in the States, that I have exactly the reputation that I would wish to have. And that is that people like me as a good entertainer, and they don't rate me too high, which always irritates and embarrasses me. I don't want to be seen as another Conrad and so on.

Interviewer: How do you feel when you've finished a book?

le Carré: Unsatisfied, always—and that's really what gets me on to the next one. I feel I've been to the limits of my talent and that I've seen what doesn't lie beyond and so I want to get going straight away on something else. This new book in particular was three years in the writing, and when I began I'd never even been to Southeast Asia.

Interviewer: How long did you spend doing research in Southeast Asia?

le Carré: About eighteen months to two years, I think. I went originally just because I'd finished *Tinker, Tailor* and was in the same unhappy state of feeling restless and unsatisfied. I thought it was time I got off my European backside and saw something I'd never seen before, which was war and Southeast Asia—Conrad territory. So that was the first trip. On that trip I was lucky enough to fall in with some journalists. Anyway I'd thought of making my main character a journalist, because one has to have an eye of some kind, and from then on I continued to commute. At the end of eighteen months I had a mass of material and one character and an idea for a story but really nothing more than that. Simply to emerge with a story from that experience was a great relief.

Interviewer: How ironically did you mean the title, *The Honourable Schoolboy*?
le Carré: Well, he's an honorable man but not a mature one. And he declined to think out his problems very much. He preferred blind service to independent thought, and so in that way Jerry (Gerald Westerby) always was something of a baby. Honorable? Well, he was trying to be.

Interviewer: You have enough money to live anywhere you want. Why do you choose England?
le Carré: Well, because it's my home, really, and because it's where my material is, the people. I do understand the English jungle, or I feel I do, the social jungle. I know the voices, and I know the vocabulary and I know the choreography of English society which is very entertaining as a framework for novels. I've always dwelt a little bit on class in English society. It's very useful, a very spicy little bit of the social comedy. Within the Circus, for instance, there's a class structure that's very clearly observed. And English manners, the lethal gentleness of British administrators sometimes. I love all that, and I couldn't imagine it from some tax haven like Ireland or while sitting in the south of France. I know I would just go flat. There's much about Britain that drives me absolutely crazy but that's also the grit in the oyster I think.

Interviewer: What more do you want from life?
le Carré: More books, really. Just more books. And although it sounds pious, I would like to get better as a writer. I would like as the Germans say to study myself and to improve, to become perhaps more sheer, in some ways to reduce, in other ways to concentrate the scope as it were. I would like to write one book which ten or twelve years later I could read and think was good.

The Secret Life of John le Carré

Godfrey Hodgson / 1977

Reprinted from the *Washington Post*, 9 October 1977, pp. E1, E6. Copyright © *Washington Post*. Reprinted by permission.

John le Carré's latest novel, The Honourable Schoolboy, *is reviewed opposite. Its theme is the one le Carré has made his own: The intellectual complexities and moral ambiguities of the secret world of intelligence services. Its two principal characters, George Smiley, who has been promoted to put the British intelligence back together after a disastrous Soviet penetration, and Jerry Westerby, the agent whose cover is that of a hardbitten war correspondent, are enriched and developed. The location is new and brilliantly described: Hong Kong and Southeast Asia in the twilight of the Vietnam war. Godfrey Hodgson, who has known le Carré since they were students together at Oxford, talked to the writer in his London home last week about craftsmanship, morality, and the secret world:*

Interviewer: When I called up I was told you were supposed to have started your new book yesterday. That suggests you're someone who can work to a timetable. How do you set about starting a new book? What comes first: theme, characters, location?

le Carré: What comes first is the industrial waste from the previous book, always. What I will do to start with is put together the notes, the backs of envelopes, and all the stuff, and close my mind to everything else.

It begins always with a couple of characters, I find. And one of the characters in this case was a fellow I wanted to fit into *The Honourable Schoolboy* and couldn't. So he was really industrial waste from *Tinker, Tailor, Soldier, Spy*. And I'm very lucky at the moment, because each book as it closes provides me with a springboard in structural terms. I mean we know Smiley is out in the cold again; that the s—ts have taken over in the Circus; the Anglo-American link has been reforged; and that the Smiley-Karla confrontation can be extended.

41

I have come to think of *Tinker, Tailor* and this book and the next two—as I think it will be—as a single continuing novel,[1] so I really am as excited as I hope my readers are to know exactly what will become of the Smiley-Karla relationship.

Interviewer: Do you begin to perceive the resolution of that?
le Carré: I do in geographical terms, yes. I think I know where their last encounter will be.

Interviewer: Let me guess: Is it Washington?
le Carré: (Laughs) No. *Nein.*

Interviewer: Critics keep writing that you must inevitably someday leave the secret world. You did actually once do that. . . .
le Carré: I did once do that, and it was, as far as the trade is concerned, a disaster. I honestly believe that critics will gradually come round to what the public has long recognized, that the spy novel is as flexible, as valid a theme in our time as any other major theme, as valid as the love story. I think it's the critics' problem, not mine.

Interviewer: Is the secret world for you a model of all human systems and relationships?
le Carré: Yes. For me, it's a microcosm of all institutional behavior, and of the ever-repeated dilemma which overcomes individuals when they submit their talent for institutional exploitation.

Interviewer: So it's no different from what happens to a man when he works. . . .
le Carré: (Interrupting) . . . for a newspaper. Or a big corporation. I know from readers' letters that much of what the man in the street gets out of my books has nothing to do with secret services, it has to do with the way he sees life in his own office. He says, "Yeah, it really is like that, it's a question of kissing ass, making secret compacts, looking over one's shoulder all the time."

---

1. le Carré did not write the fourth novel in this cycle. *Tinker, Tailor, Soldier, Spy* (1974), *The Honourable Schoolboy* (1977), and *Smiley's People* (1980) were collected as *The Quest for Karla* in 1982.

Interviewer: And yet you've spent less time in offices than almost anyone I know?

le Carré: That's right. I was free from that at the age of thirty-one. I think I was so much of a striver myself that the short time I spent trying to advance through an institution left an indelible impression on me.

Interviewer: There are two pairs of themes which seem to be almost obsessive in your books. One is truth and deceit, the other is loyalty and betrayal. Why? Is this buried in your personal experience?

le Carré: Well, the preoccupation with deceit does, I think, very much relate to the way my late papa lived. We all knew that for, I think, the last thirty years he was an undischarged bankrupt. But he managed to keep an office in Jermyn Street going, and a house in the country, and ran a couple of cars, and raised credit. He lived dangerously, and he lived a very dangerous love life. As kids we were very aware of that, and we knew that we couldn't tell this to that person or that to this person, whether it was money or love. But he had such a wonderful plausibility, and always such a wonderful potential, that he drew on his credit and his charm indefinitely. So my brother and I, we followed. We used to sing together, "my old man says, follow the band. . . ."

I think there is a theme in my work, to do with deceit, which says almost as one critic put it recently, to act is to betray. That the individual identity is really irreconcilable with any collective behavior. And that's probably just the posture of the outsider.

Interviewer: But you seem to be saying, with Westerby in *The Honourable Schoolboy*, that a man can arrive at some kind of truthfulness through action, even though in so doing he betrays, perhaps, his mother, his girlfriend, his wife, his superiors and even the organization he's acting for?

le Carré: You see, all of these people, Smiley, Jerry, or the girl, Lizzie, they're all looking for their own moral center in some way. They all believe that in some way they're doing good. Smiley believes that he is sublimating his own personal feelings for the general good. Jerry believes that in sublimating his feelings to Smiley he too is acting for the general good. The girl believes in true feeling.

Interviewer: While at the same time, she's a tart.

le Carré: That's right. The moral centers shift, so that by the end of the story Smiley is appallingly tortured by the fact that he has deployed friendship so as to bring about someone's destruction.

Interviewer: There's a conflict in your work which I find interesting. You are offering as a moral justification the work itself. Smiley, or Westerby, or other characters, achieve justification because of their faithfulness not to wives, girlfriends, or anything else, but to the task itself. At the same time you're saying, in the most biting and penetrating way, that this particular kind of work is almost useless, and largely pernicious.

le Carré: You are absolutely right. You've nailed the paradox. But I function at one level when I write, and that's the level at which I convert observation into fable and narrative, and try to draw stories out of a morass of what we all know to be paradoxical information. We are divided. Those of us who've been on nodding terms with these outfits have learned, very seriously, to wonder whether they're any bloody good at all. But if they are good, if they're going to stand up and be counted against the KGB, which without doubt is a ruthless, messy, vile, and very effective organization, are we going to feel safe with them? So that I don't think I'm being slippery when I say that the paradox is one we all share.

Interviewer: It's the moral problem of the man who has to be a martyr for a religion he doesn't believe in?

le Carré: But when we look at the heathen, we run back and take new faith. However liberal and doubtful we may be there is absolutely no doubt that world communism is not something I wish my children to be subjected to.

The novelist in me is always wrestling with this problem at an artistic level. You see, I have to invent a kernel of great professional competence, which is Smiley. There has to be, at the romantic level, a degree of excellence. It's something we all want, as readers, and without it you get perilously close to farce and chaos. Which perhaps may be the true version of secret service work. We've certainly seen that in the Watergate hearings. Farce, chaos, the goldmakers, the charlatans, the fantasists. We had a whole parade of them at Watergate.

Interviewer: You seem to have an attitude to the United States that is perhaps a classically European one: You seem to suspect the U.S. of representing, with immense power, dangerous value systems. Your Americans seem almost to be zombies, without apparently any personal moral or intellectual dilemmas of their own.

le Carré: Well, the American intelligence outfit as I see it in the book actually represents two kinds of Americans. There's the tweedy, Yaley sort, who's

Martello, the Allen Dulles *école*, you know: "We're elitist chaps, used to privilege, so it's no problem for us to exercise these rather extraordinary powers." And then there are the gray men, who should be feeding computers with information from the satellites. These are the figures one saw around the edges of the Vietnam War, who had all sorts of pretty words for "kill." They're scary.

Both Jerry and Smiley, I think, have the same feeling about Americans. It's not just a condescending European view. Both of them have a rather shameful respect for the fact that the mantle of power has moved west. As Macmillan said, that we may have the knowledge, but no longer the power. That we're the last of the Greeks. It's a Gaullist view too.

Jerry doesn't care for large-scale theories, but he did dimly recognize that he belonged to the class that had thrown away the game. And that he in some indirect way was responsible. It's not just a question of feeling that the power has gone to the wrong chaps, but also a question of feeling that one has f—ed it up.

And Smiley also is very much concerned with *raison d'état*. He knows that one must go to where the power is. He says to Jerry very firmly, either you're in or you're out. He says in effect: "I belong to the generation that was born into a debtors' prison, and it's our luck that we've got to spend our lives buying our way out." This sense of generation guilt is very strong in the book.

Interviewer: You seem to portray the Americans as agents, and not also as patients; to miss the tormenting sense of impotence and limitations which have been part of the life of this kind of American in this generation.
le Carré: It's probably true that at the technical level I've failed to bring that kind of sympathy to the American, but there is a moment when Jerry meets a CIA man in the field who holds out his hands, and says something like: "I'd like you to shake me by the hand, we've just become a second-class power."

Interviewer: You very accurately make that kind of American contemptuous and almost racist about "the Brits." . . .
le Carré: That's right, that's something we've all met. And I think maybe I failed to dramatize something that came over to me very strongly during my tours of Southeast Asia, and that was that the Americans and the Brits have been drawn far closer together by the collapse of the Southeast Asian adventure. Because the Americans learned then a lesson about the limitations of power.

Interviewer: You're also saying something, it seems to me, that is expressed in *Ecclesiastes*, where it says, "the race is not to the swift, nor the battle to the strong." That personal excellence is unrelated to success.
le Carré: I believe that is so, yes.

Interviewer: And I believe that, in general, Americans tend not to believe this, but to believe that one does well by doing good.
le Carré: Yes. Perhaps Americans also believe that the man who has succeeded, almost by definition, will become a good man. It's part of the presidential image.

Interviewer: And you don't believe that?
le Carré: I think it has yet to be demonstrated.

Interviewer: Let me ask you something which is very topical in the United States at the moment: you present a lot of the journalists in your book as having worked for intelligence services. What is it that you're saying?
le Carré: Well, as a practical matter, it is surely an open secret that any journalist worth his salt knows the identity of the heads of the secret services in the areas where he functions. It's also an open secret that there's a sort of mutual dependence. A journalist is frequently able to tough his way into an interview which would be denied to anyone with any other sort of ascription. So it seems to me to be idiotic to imagine that these things didn't go on. What's happening is that the public is catching up consciously with what, subconsciously, it knew all along.

Hong Kong Was a "Halfway House"

Michael Barber / 1978

Reprinted from *Newsagent and Bookshop*, 30 November 1978, pp. 22–23.
Copyright © *Newsagent and Bookshop*.

Although he still regards big cities as "occupied territory," John le Carré has decided for private and professional reasons to try and build a London life for himself and his family. We talked in the study of his house in Hampstead. On the wall beside his desk he has scribbled these lines by Hippocrates: "Whoever does not reach the capacity of common people and fails to make them listen misses the mark."

Interviewer: Mr. le Carré, you once pointed out that spies spent a lot of their time pretending to be characters "outside of themselves." Isn't there an obvious analogy here with writers?

le Carré: Yes, I've certainly drawn that parallel in my own mind. It's part of a writer's profession, as it's part of a spy's profession, to prey on the community to which he's attached, to take away information—often in secret—and to translate that into intelligence for his masters, whether it's his readership or his spy masters. And I think that both professions are perhaps rather lonely.

Interviewer: Would you also agree that both thrive on tension?

le Carré: Well, certainly I don't think that there are very many good writers who don't live without a sense of tension. If they haven't got one immediately available to them, then they usually manage to manufacture it in their private lives. But I think the real tension lies in the relationship between what you might call the pursuer and his quarry, whether it's the writer or the spy. Graham Greene once referred to a chip of ice that has to be in the writer's heart. And that is the strain: that you must abstract from relationships and yet at the same time engage in them. There you have, I think, the real metaphysical relationship between the writer and the spy.

47

Interviewer: I think Eric Ambler[1] once said that there is a criminal and a policeman in all of us, and that this could account for the popularity of spy fiction and allied genres. Would you agree?

le Carré: I think there's something much more fundamental at work at the moment. We have learnt in recent years to translate almost all of political life in terms of conspiracy. And the spy novel, as never before really, has come into its own. There is such cynicism about the orthodox forms of government as they are offered to the public that we believe almost nothing at its face value. Now, somehow or other the politicians try to convey to us that this suspicion is misplaced. But we know better than that. And until we have a better relationship between private performance and the public truth, as was demonstrated with Watergate, we as the public are absolutely right to remain suspicious and contemptuous, even, of the secrecy and the misinformation which is the digest of our news. So I think that the spy novel encapsulates this public wariness about political behaviour and about the set-up, the fix of society. And I think also, in entertainment terms, it makes a kind of fable about forces we do believe in the West are stacked against us.

Interviewer: Is it true that you once compared writing your novels to making a jam roll?—you open the pastry out, spread the jam, and then roll it up.

le Carré: Well, if I did, I'm already beginning to regret it! But I think as a rough principle I always begin with one character, and then perhaps two, and they seem to be in conflict with each other. "The cat sat on the mat" is not a story. "The cat sat on the dog's mat *is* a story." And I have a sense of atmosphere, the environment in which I want to set them, and a sense of how the ending will be. From there the story takes over by itself. But the layer cake you refer to—yes, I like to lead the story forward, and therefore the reader forward, on a whole variety of levels, and try to make all these levels then converge and pay off at the end.

Interviewer: So rather than impose a plot on your characters, you follow Scott Fitzgerald's dictum: "character is action"?

le Carré: Very much so. For instance in *The Honourable Schoolboy* I began with two basic characters. George Smiley, who's a constant companion in these books, and then somebody who had a walk-on part in *Tinker, Tailor, Soldier,*

1. (1909–1998); British spy novelist whose books included *The Mask of the Dimitrios* (1939).

Spy, and who now takes a major role, that's Jerry Westerby. And I had planted in Jerry's past in the previous book the fact that he had a Far Eastern background. And so I set off for the Far East with those two people and a rough idea of the evanescence of the western presence in South East Asia, and beyond that, I felt, I had no preconceptions. And I found myself referring to Jerry and George as "my secret sharers." So it was an act of complicity, I suppose, between myself and the characters that we finally drew the story out of their motivation.

Interviewer: Was Jerry's Far Eastern background a happy accident?
le Carré: No, it was what you might call an inspired accident. In laying the foundations of some of these minor characters I've tried always to give them such a variety of qualifications that I could pick them up later if I wanted to— by actually pulling their card out of a card index that I keep—and then perhaps turn them from two-dimensional into three-dimensional characters. And I knew toward the end of *Tinker, Tailor* that I wanted a change of scene. And I think that by scribbling in those few lines that Jerry was an old Asian hand and so on I was setting that up for myself later. . . . But I loved him as a character in *Tinker, Tailor*. Just the few pages I gave him, I thought he was a winner.

Interviewer: I was very struck by the way your Chinese speak English in *The Honourable Schoolboy*. You must have an excellent ear for idiom.
le Carré: I believe that is something I do have. I think I was born with two, for a writer, lucky skills. One is a very good ear for voice and also a very retentive ear, so that I can recall both accent and words for a long time afterwards. And the other is a wary retention of certain detail—topography, rooms, furniture, and so on.

Interviewer: Are you a good mimic?
le Carré: It's said of me, yes. And I am a linguist, which helps.

Interviewer: Has this had any effect on your style?
le Carré: I think it certainly has. And more particularly having a largely German-oriented education has made me very responsive to nineteenth-century German literature. The predominant form of the lately-emerging novel in Germany then was what they called *Bildungsroman*, a novel of education, in which a single character was taken through a variety of rooms, as you might say, a variety of encounters and experiences, and brought out at the other end

a changed and generally a morally-reformed figure. If that didn't happen there was an apocalypse of some kind and he was destroyed. And I think that one could say that to a great extent that form is something I've clung to in my own novels. Generally speaking, they are finally about one person.

Interviewer: I think you've acknowledged that you sell far better in Europe and America than in Britain. Yet unlike some English writers one could name, you make no concessions to foreign readers. Indeed, your delight in our esoteric social institutions seems almost provocative!

le Carré: Yes, the question of the Englishness of my books and yet their exportability fascinates me too and I've come up with no real solution to it. Funnily enough I had my French translator on the phone only this morning asking me to explain various cricketing terms I'd used. The only explanation I could offer is to refer back to the classical form of the detective story, the country-house scene, Hercule Poirot pointing to the suspect and so on: that English society does offer a particular comedy of manners which lends itself very well to suspense. If you know that the butler was in the wrong room at the wrong time that's already an exciting thing because the norms and forms of English behaviour are so rigid that transgression is the beginning of suspense. Whereas if you were writing about a hippie commune in San Francisco, nobody would know what rules applied—who should be sleeping with whom, who should be feeding the baby and so on. In an English, domestic, *Upstairs, Downstairs* situation, everyone knows what the ground rules are and the foreign reader will accept this. Now, if you describe a Secret Service and impose upon it the same ground rules of behaviour as you would upon an English country house, you quickly get the reader with you. So that these are bits of ammunition which are available to an English writer, and properly used, are pure gold in my experience.

Interviewer: Was the Circus always going to be a constant in your novels?

le Carré: Not at the beginning. But then as I became more ambitious, I thought that it would in time work itself into a very beautiful microcosm of English behaviour and English society altogether.

Interviewer: So when, in *The Honourable Schoolboy*, Smiley says that the Circus must stir itself because "Not to produce was not to trade, and not to trade was to die," you wanted to make a point about Britain today?

le Carré: Yes, that was exactly the analogy I tried to make. It's very dangerous to talk of one's symbolism, but I felt that at the end of *Tinker, Tailor* I had shown a Secret Service totally betrayed and in pieces on the floor. At the beginning of *The Honourable Schoolboy* in comes Smiley to sweep up the stable and get things going. And he has to breathe vigour into a completely dismayed and disoriented and poorly-equipped outfit. And the parallels between our economy and the English *cafard* and what was going on in the Circus and what Smiley was trying to get on the move, they were irresistible to me.

Interviewer: Is it true that the C.I.A. have adopted some of your Circus jargon—lamplighters, scalphunters, etc?

le Carré: I'm told that they've definitely adopted the word "mole" for what they used to call a "sleeper," which is a long-term penetration agent who does nothing until he's activated. It may be that they also use other expressions that have appeared in my books. If so, I'm flattered.

Interviewer: Up until *The Honourable Schoolboy* all your books had been set in Britain or Europe. Why the shift to South-East Asia?

le Carré: Well, I'd never seen war. South-East Asia was the area of conflict. And for better or worse I've been involved in the description of political conflict. Also, I was very aware of a feeling of professional menopause. I felt that I needed new horizons for my own self as well as my work. And it was a wonderful challenge to take on a completely new theatre of life and experience and try to fit it into fictional form.

Interviewer: When did you first realise that you had a book on your hands?

le Carré: When we hit Hong Kong. I knew then that I could exploit that last colony—*Borrowed Time, Borrowed Place* as Richard Hughes[2] called it with his book—and make it a point of reference if I was going to step out into the exotica of Cambodia and Laos and Vietnam. I think a sense of manners towards the reader intervenes here. I believe it's possible to be too exotic in a novel to the point where the Western, round-eyed reader is simply lost, where his standard of comparison is taken away from him. And Hong Kong was a

---

2. Australian journalist based in Asia; author or *Borrowed Time, Borrowed Place* (1968) and *Foreign Devil* (1972).

kind of half-way house. When Jerry was in Hong Kong, you knew that in a way he was at least putting one foot back in the world of western manners.

Interviewer: You referred earlier to the "evanescence of the Western presence in South-East Asia." Presumably you had a ringside seat at this?
le Carré: Yes, that immediately became apparent. I realised that if I was going to set my book in South-East Asia, it was already certain to be a historical novel. And when I left Phnom Penh—when Jerry left Phnom Penh—we both had the feeling that we would never return.

Interviewer: When you took Richard Hughes and turned him into old Craw, did you realise that he'd already appeared, as Dikko Henderson, in Fleming's *You Only Live Twice*?
le Carré: Yes, but only after I'd written to him about my own plans. I said, "I propose to libel you in my book. I'm going to have an old and not completely abstemious Australian journalist at the center. Do you mind?" He wrote back and said, "My boy, libel me to the hilt!" and then reminded me that Fleming had done the same.

Interviewer: In your early novels you seemed to imply that no society was worth defending by the kind of methods you had set out to expose. Have your opinions hardened since then?
le Carré: I think they have. I don't know whether it's age or maturity, but I certainly find myself committed more and more to the looser forms of Western democracy at any price. And I've become more and more disenchanted about the possibility of understanding with the Soviet Union as it's constructed at the moment.

le Carré's Circus: Lamplighters, Moles and Others of That Ilk

Paul Vaughan / 1979

Reprinted from *The Listener*, 13 September 1979, pp. 339–40. *Kaleidoscope* (Radio 4). Copyright © *The Listener*. Reprinted by permission.

le Carré: I turned down movie offers for *Tinker, Tailor, Soldier, Spy* when it first came out because I thought that, as a film, the condensation would be impossible. Then the idea came up—first, incidentally, with independent television—that we should do what in those days was quite a new venture—a mini-series from the book of six or seven hours. A very distinguished and lovable scriptwriter worked on it, and I think he would be the first to agree now that he didn't do his best and I didn't like the work. I exercised my right to decline the deal and we sent the money back and waited.

Then we started again on the same rather tentative basis with Arthur Hopcraft, John Irvin, the director, and the great Alec Guinness, and it was through the mystery of Guinness that, for me at least, the thing really became attractive. I hasten to say I still couldn't envisage it at this stage, but I know that when we sat down with Guinness that first time for lunch—myself and Irvin and Hopcraft and Jonathan Powell, the producer—we were simply fascinated, first of all by the innate modesty of the man which in itself is evidence of an extraordinary presence. His capacity for self-effacement, his capacity for adaptation! He is so flexible and listens so closely to the wind while he's talking to you that even with four people round him he seems to be a different person to each one. Whether it was Smiley or not at that stage seemed almost irrelevant. One knew one was dealing with an absolutely hypnotic actor, which is terribly important for television and terribly important for this rather slow-moving type of drama. Guinness's acting is like clockwork. It's like opening up a watch and every tiny little piece works so beautifully. And I think, from that moment on, we knew that we were dealing with something that was potentially very exciting.

Interviewer: Was any violence done to the plot to get it into the seven episodes of the series?

53

le Carré: There were hideous problems from the start with the amount of flashback which the novel used. We had to unfold the Swiss roll and slice it differently, and that is something *I* could not have done. I was much too close to the material and my own synopses never had the lucidity of Hopcraft's. He saw a way through very quickly, and I think he broke the back of the thing with his first synopsis. So I believe people will not be aware of the rearrangement of the information until they make an intellectual comparison. The whole story is there but it's just arranged differently now, it's re-orchestrated.

Interviewer: You weren't, I suppose, in the same position that I believe Raymond Chandler was known to be in, where aspects of plots of his novels were suddenly revealed to him that he hadn't seen before? There's a story about him having a telegram from Howard Hawks, saying, "Who did kill the butler?" And he sent a reply saying, "I'm damned if I know!"[1]

le Carré: I'm certainly in the position of not quite remembering how the plot worked, and of having, at times, the uneasy feeling that it didn't. Part of the book's purpose is to have an extremely labyrinthine plot and so I think one can be forgiven, two or three books later, for not remembering the intricacies of it. And I have great resistance to rereading my own work.

Interviewer: Why this resistance?

le Carré: It embarrasses me really. Sometimes the memory of them, or reading a few pages of them, will act as a springboard, an incentive to do better things. But it's so much a part of a writer's ambition, I think, to believe that he will finally write something he's prepared to be buried with, that looking back, looking over my shoulder, always leaves me with a very uncomfortable feeling of mortality.

Interviewer: I'm interested in what you say about the labyrinthine nature of the book, and that this was intentional. This aspect could be said about most, if not all, of your novels—that you did intend them to have this very convoluted structure. Is that right?

le Carré: Yes. I think it's part of the tension and part of the music of the books, perhaps, to restate repeatedly the conspiratorial thesis that nothing is

---

1. The exchange—possibly apocryphal—was about the death of the chauffeur in *The Big Sleep*.

ever quite what it seems to be—that you enter one room only to find another door ahead of you, and so on. And I think this maze effect is frequently an end in itself to me. I certainly am aware, sometimes, that if I were reading this book, I would not be able to hold all the threads in my hand. And one of the functions of Smiley—and this is a very important thing about casting—is to act as a central intellect in whom the reader has so much confidence. When Smiley is becoming analytical and intuitive about things you more or less leave the reasoning to him. And I think that that is frequently the thing that will take one through an otherwise impossibly complex plot in a story of investigation of this sort. The twists are really quite often there for their own sake because they keep the ground moving all the time; you know that nowhere is safe. Just as Smiley's own house isn't safe; one of the most dangerous places for him is home.

Interviewer: Could I take you back to the point at which this book was actually written—1974. What, in fact, made you want to write this book? You had diverged slightly from your usual conventional path, you'd got away from writing books about espionage and treachery and you'd written *The Naive and Sentimental Lover*.

le Carré: I was extremely hurt by the awful reception which *The Naive and Sentimental Lover* got at the time. It would be idle to pretend that I was not. *Tinker, Tailor* was the most difficult book I ever wrote and I did destroy two versions of it in despair before I came up with one that I thought worked. Perhaps the intellectual thrust of it and the labyrinthine plot and the extremely inward complexity of the final solution—the way the "mole" spy had operated, and so on—perhaps all of these things, in a way, are attributable to that rather desperate mood I was in, needing to hack out some solution to a very confused time in my life. I did decide, secretly, that I would write three books which formed a crude trilogy—*Tinker, Tailor*, then *The Honourable Schoolboy*, and the third one which I've just completed. For good trade reasons one doesn't like to announce one's going to write a trilogy. If the book's a flop you're landed with the other two, or you have to crawl out of the tunnel. Another reason is that there is a resistance from people, feeling they're coming in in the middle of a trilogy or even buying the last one in a trilogy. So one has to be jolly careful. But I thought I would write those three, which I've now done, and then I would hang Smiley's boots up, at least for a while.

Interviewer: How did you first come to invent Smiley?

le Carré: I don't really know. But I think that there was one prototype originally, certainly in appearance there was one man who had his features, his looks and many of his mannerisms—particularly the one of removing his spectacles and polishing them on the inside of the fat end of his tie. "He was one of London's meek who do not inherit the earth"—an absolutely forgettable man, the most forgettable man I ever met, who was also very intelligent. I worked with him for a while in the Civil Service. Then, I think gradually, as with most of one's characters, he becomes a vessel into which you put other things, and I think Smiley changes very much from book to book. But he's the reader's companion in a way. I find from readers' letters and talking to people that he is that figure in whom they feel able to trust. They can put their hand in his and he leads them through the story.

Interviewer: I'm always very impressed by the way all the Civil Service jargon and all the procedural detail in your books seems to be so accurate.

le Carré: I don't know how accurate it is but it's very important to me with characters, situations, plots to preserve the air of banality. It is, I think, a very important factor of storytelling that the nearer you can bring the fantasy to the reality, the more people are willing to swallow the fantasy. Authenticity is frightfully boring but credibility is what novel writing is about, and plausibility; if you put two spies on a bus they're much more attractive to the general reader than if you put them in a jet aeroplane. I do place great emphasis on keeping the humdrum alive.

Interviewer: How do you know about all the arcana of espionage practice, the famous phrases about scalphunters and babysitters and lamplighters and pavement artists?

le Carré: Those are all made up. I have since met a number of intelligence officers and ex-intelligence officers—mainly American—and I'm gratified to learn that some of my jargon has gone into their language.

Interviewer: In your books there always seems to be a sort of international community of spies—rather like the kind of faintly fraternal relationship that used to exist on the Western Front—they're all in this together. The Russian agents and the English agents know they have certain aims in common; it just happens that one is on one side and one is on the other.

This always seems to me to be highly credible. Do you think this accounts for the sort of moral queasiness that I sometimes feel is at the centre of your books—that black can suddenly become white?

le Carré: I think it's an unresolved dilemma which lies about in the books, often rather like static electricity, and is part of the tension of them. There is a constant moral ambiguity as there is in most things in our lives. It resides in the basic paradox that we are in the process of doing things in defence of our society which may very well produce a society which is not worth defending; we're constantly asking ourselves what is the price we can pay in order to preserve a society, yet what sort of society is preservable? I think these are irreconcilable problems, but I am myself absolutely satisfied that, by and large, the West has a better record. I think it's quite wrong to say, now, from what we know of the KGB and its methods, that both sides in fact use the same methods. We have, occasionally, in certain areas, gone absolutely overboard, as the Americans did in Vietnam, but, by and large, our moral preoccupations are considerably more dignified and real, I'm sure, than those of the other side. But it doesn't make the dilemma any the less for those who are actually having to do the dirty work.

Interviewer: In *Tinker, Tailor, Soldier, Spy*, one bit of moral bedrock in the book is the prep school where Prideaux has ended up and where the right kind of values are being propagated. Prideaux tells one of the boys that England stands for all that is best; on one side there are little men in uniforms and on the other there's a civilisation we don't really trust—I forget the words you used—but it means America.

le Carré: There is a very difficult problem when you write about the British engaging in Cold War situations because they have this enormous ally who really does the hard work these days, and we trot along far, far behind. If you're using British society as the microcosm for your Cold War story, you have somehow to place the Americans in the scheme of things, and one of the most convenient ways of dealing with that problem is to make them unpopular and therefore take them out of the picture. And I'm afraid I've been guilty of that tactic in order to leave the weight of the story with the British. I did that in *The Spy Who Came in From the Cold*, as well—that leaves the reader with the illusion that the British are fighting their own wars, which is quite untrue. I think there is, also—in all my later books, anyway—a strong line of simplistic, wishful, chauvinist thinking in one or another character, people who, for very honourable reasons, often for reasons of their own natural intellectual limitations, are loyal, decent, unashamedly patriotic blokes, like Jerry Westerby in *The Honourable Schoolboy* or Jim Prideaux in *Tinker, Tailor, Soldier, Spy*. People who have almost deliberately foreshortened their critical faculties in order to believe their country right or wrong, and those chaps, ironically, always get the worst drubbing in the story, because you simply cannot cease to criticise, however noble one's reasons.

Interviewer: It's really betrayal which is at the centre of your books, isn't it?
le Carré: Yes. I think it's more to do with corporate and individual loyalty, the conflict between the two. Ann Smiley betrays her husband; she is quite definitely loyal to a notion of the way she should live. She says that her feelings guide her in these directions, and where others might simply leer or lust, she does, she acts, and that is a more honest way to behave than to live a repressive and voyeuristic sort of life. Other people have been betrayed in my books by nationhood. They've invested their loyalty in their country, blindly; they've often been brought up to one ethic and found themselves landed with another, which is a form of historical betrayal which occurs to very many people—people who were bombing Berlin in 1945 could easily have been trying to save Berlin in the Airlift in 1948. It's quite amazing the betrayals which historical reversal thrusts upon us, and so very many of my characters are the victims of an accelerated history that we live through. They are left-over men, the no-man of no-man's land, who have tried and simply become exhausted, have tried to toe the line and been defeated. It's very much betrayal of human values, personal, individual values, in favour of some corporate necessity, and there is the corporate necessity turning round and—as P. G. Wodehouse would say—"socking us on the back of the head with a stuffed eel-skin."

Interviewer: Is something like that behind the following passage from *Tinker, Tailor, Soldier, Spy*? It's the moment where Guillam finally realises who the traitor is:

> Now that he saw, he knew. "X" was more than his model, he was his inspiration, the torch-bearer of a certain kind of antiquated romanticism, a notion of English calling which—for the very reason that it was vague and understated and elusive—had made sense of Guillam's life till now. In that moment, Guillam felt not merely betrayed, but orphaned. His suspicions, his resentments for so long turned outwards

on the real world—on his women, his attempted loves—now swung upon the Circus and the failed magic which had formed his faith. With all his force, he shoved open the door and sprang inside, gun in hand.

le Carré: Yes. That is a good part of it. Connie Sachs, in the same book, also has some good lines on the same subject when she says to Smiley, as Smiley is leaving and Connie is drunk, as usual, "Poor loves," she says, "empire babies born to rule an empire and what are you left with?" I think that I belong almost to the last of that particular generation who still, after the war, were being advised by their careers masters at public school to go and govern India, Kenya, the Sudan or where you will. We really were brought up to believe that we were the best and the brightest, that we'd inherited the mantle of postwar imperialism, that we were the people for whom the war had been fought and now the earth was ours and we had a great duty to run it decently. And, of course, within fifteen years of that, we realised that our problem was not to run the world but to come to terms with the fact of the world running us.

Interviewer: You are part of the post-imperialist school of fiction!
le Carré: I think I've got a foot in each camp and that's how we reached this kind of headache.

Interviewer: In your next book we reach the end of the trilogy and conceivably the end of Smiley's professional career. What's going to happen after that? Is it too soon to ask you what your next book will be?
le Carré: At the moment I'm drifting between Cornwall and Hampstead, slouching around with my hands in my pockets and my head bowed, kicking at stones, wondering what to do. I'm going off to America, I've got publishing things to do, but it's a rare and wonderful moment in my life that I honestly have not the least idea what I shall do next. The paper looks very blank and I feel quite tired but life's very good.

The Secret World of John le Carré

Miriam Gross / 1980

Interviewer: Of all your characters it is Smiley who has gradually emerged as the central figure, and in your new book you reinforce this by using his name in the title.[1] What drew you to this kind of unglamorous, low-key hero?

le Carré: Well, in the first place his age is important. I wanted somebody who was part of the seamless transition—as it looked to someone of my generation—from the hot war to the Cold War. And that meant twenty years ago, when I started writing about him, he was already middle-aged. I also wanted somebody who was socially rather a misfit.

I think my own background inclined me towards someone without any very obvious class origins. On Smiley's first appearance in the very first book he is described as a man who travelled without labels in the guard's van of the social express. And I knew that I would relate best to somebody of that kind of floating nature.

At the same time he belongs to a generation—it was the generation of the traitors, too—who felt particularly strongly that one must commit oneself one way or another, that there is no middle way. And *faute de mieux* he has committed himself to the Establishment cause—although I don't think it's enough for him. He has a sense of decency but he's not sure where to invest it.

Interviewer: Most of your books seem to take place in a sort of grey area, morally. I think it's rather difficult to tell from them where you stand yourself.

le Carré: If I knew exactly where I stood I wouldn't write. I do believe, reluctantly, that we must combat Communism. Very decisively. Of course, our own engagement in the Cold War is a rather well-kept British secret. I don't

1. *Smiley's People.*

think many British people are aware of the extent to which we are harnessed to the anti-Communist effort. Perhaps Mrs Thatcher[2] is making us more aware of it.

That doesn't mean I necessarily think that the goodies are all on one side and the baddies on the other. I detest dogma, institutionalised prejudice, even party politics. And even if the baddies were all on one side, I think Smiley is far too aware of the element of humanity in everybody to be able to hate them as they perhaps should be hated.

His engagement against Communism is really an intellectual one. I think he stands where I stand: he feels that to pit yourself against any "ism" is to strike a posture which is itself ideological, and therefore offensive in terms of practical decency. In practice almost any political ideology invites you to set aside your humanitarian instincts.

He's also very understanding of human fallibility: he knows that most of life is led below the water's surface, and that people are very secretive creatures—secret even from themselves. He accepts, however reluctantly, that you have to resort to very unpleasant means in order to preserve society, though he sometimes wonders how much you can do in the name of that society and feel sure that it is still worth preserving. And that dilemma remains unsolved to the end.

Interviewer: And do you put things into your novels which you think couldn't happen in real life?
le Carré: I think the plots all work. But the one thing which is extremely difficult to dramatise is the persistent quality of human incompetence—particularly in British administration. I don't think *The Spy Who Came in From the Cold* could happen, because I don't believe that it's ever possible to operate such a clean conspiracy, where all the pieces fit together.

Whether it's the Thorpe affair[3] or the Blunt affair,[4] if you have to choose between conspiracy or cock-up, my instinct is to go for the cock-up every time. And in writing, one has to tread a very fine line between the reality of incompetence and the reader's very human wish to visit a world where logic and action have a reasonable relationship to each other.

2. Margaret Thatcher, British Prime Minister from 1979 to 1990.
3. In 1976 M.P. Jeremy Thorpe's career was ruined by charges that he had engaged in a homosexual relationship.
4. Sir Anthony Blunt's long-time activities as a Soviet spy were revealed in 1979.

We all know how hilariously frail most decision-making is, and anyone who has been party to the British variety—as revealed in the Crossman Diaries,[5] for instance—knows that outrageous factors can play overwhelming parts. This is the most difficult thing to get into a book, at any rate into a book of the genre to which I contribute.

Smiley operates in defiance both of incompetence, and of the latent treachery which is always around in that world. If you hire people to lie for the country, you shouldn't be too surprised if now and then they lie to you as well. Smiley understands that. So do I. So, after the succession of recent exposures in the States, does the American public; and they don't like it one bit.

Interviewer: When you wrote *Tinker, Tailor*, did you have a real-life traitor, like Philby for instance, in mind?
le Carré: I had all the traitors in mind, in a sense. Those who were known about. I was also taking, you might say, a didactic position, one which I took up when the *Sunday Times* Insight Team asked me to write an introduction to their Philby book back in 1968.[6]

My point then was that Philby had an innate disposition to deceive which preceded his Marxism—that his Marxism was a rationalisation, which came later. His deceitful nature derived, I suspect, from that rather horrendous father of his, St John Philby, and also from an overwhelming vanity about his own worth.

He grew up with the idea that he was born, as Connie Sachs says of Bill Haydon, as an Empire baby, to rule; and he entered a world where all his toys were being taken away by history. It seems to me that for that kind of Establishment person this is a much more cogent motive for betrayal than any half-cock pro-Stalinist Marxism which could not be seriously sustained after University.

That was what I said in my introduction, to the greater anger, at the time, of such people as Graham Greene and Hugh Trevor-Roper.[7] Greene felt I was being cheap about a man he admired. Trevor-Roper, I think, felt that I was an

5. Richard Crossman, M.P., whose *Diaries of a Cabinet Minister* (1975) revealed the inner workings of the British government.
6. Bruce Page, David Leitch, and Phillip Knightley, *Philby: The Spy Who Betrayed a Generation* (London: André Deutsch, 1968); *The Philby Conspiracy* (Garden City, N.Y.: Doubleday, 1968). le Carré's introduction was published in both editions.
7. Distinguished British historian (1914–2003) who was made a life peer in 1987.

ignoramus about pretty well everything, but in particular the political climate of the Thirties—I hadn't been there, I didn't know.

But I still believe I was right—Philby was a bent voluptuary: Come to think of it—yes, I gave that quality to Haydon, and perhaps I did pinch it from Philby.

Interviewer: What about Blunt?

le Carré: Blunt is a marginally different case, I think, because he was one of a homosexual group who were, in their own minds at least, not only a self-selecting élite, but a self-loving one as well. One forgets nowadays the extent to which homosexuality, at that period, was of itself a commitment to a secret world.

We all know that, even when they are not homosexuals, men who are locked up in smoke-filled rooms can, with time, generate absolutely nutty ideas. These people were not only vain and secretive, but a real brotherhood apart; and it's entirely understandable to me how, in the political and sexual climate of those days, they should have exerted crazy influences over one another.

There was also still enough innocence about Marxism around for people to believe that with political liberation would come sexual liberation. When the true human forces were finally released by Socialism—they reasoned—their own sexuality would be released also. It was part of their Greek dream, and it totally disregarded the bourgeois Puritanism which is at the root of Soviet Communism.

Interviewer: Were you surprised or shocked by the Blunt disclosure?

le Carré: Not surprised. The rumours had been around for years. I don't think we know the real story even now, either. I don't think we've had revelations—we've had names. Some of them most unjustly tarnished. We don't know what Blunt did, nor how he obtained his amnesty. What deal did he make with the authorities? Whisper who dares.

I was hypnotised by his television performance, and I think it made me angrier than anything I can recall in recent times.

Interviewer: Why?

le Carré: Well, for one thing it was pretty macabre to hear a self-confessed Russian spy primly taking refuge in the Official Secrets Act. But mainly I think it was his voice, the feeling that he was somehow patronising us. Telling us that because he was *this* kind of person, in *this* setting, he demanded *this* kind of credulity. His performance in *The Times* offices brought out practically all the social resentments that are still left in me.

Interviewer: What do you feel about the way life has been imitating art? It seemed amazing especially during the television showing of *Tinker, Tailor*.
le Carré: Well, I must say it scared me slightly. I don't think that I was consciously pursuing any particular original when I wrote about Bill Haydon—but it gave me a slight frisson to recall that Haydon had been a painter and given his own exhibitions at Oxford, with Jim Prideaux hanging up the pictures for him; that the two of them had quite obviously had a homosexual relationship; and that later in the story Haydon emerges as a fancier of classical drawing.

It's even stranger that in the first draft of *Tinker, Tailor* I was going to have the traitor figure as a retired member of the Circus, not an active one, and that much of the story was going to take place in his house, in a series of interrogations which reached right back to the homosexual artistic world of Oxbridge in the Thirties.

Looking back through those early drafts, I find that there were easels, collections of Old Master drawings and things dotted all over Haydon's house, and that he was an art expert as well as a former spy.

Interviewer: You said earlier that your own background inclined you towards someone like Smiley without any very obvious class origins. What was your background?
le Carré: My parents separated when I was very young and I spent most of my childhood with my father. He was a colourful and curious personality. He was the only son of religious lower-middle-class parents and he was tremendously ambitious to get out, by any means. And he did, but this landed him early in his life in fearful financial difficulties; and indeed in prison. He was a Micawber character who always managed to spend twice as much as he earned—or twice as much as he obtained.

He was a fantasist, perhaps a schizophrenic. He liked using several names. A lot of people found him magical, and as a boy, I suppose I did too. So we found ourselves, my brother and I, often living in the style of millionaire paupers.

We all knew there was absolutely no money—the bills hadn't been paid, the staff hadn't been paid—we knew there was a lot to hide: women, the past, the present.

My brother and I were the first in the family to be turned into fake gentry. We had to go to public school, willy nilly. For this my father always said that he was prepared to steal if necessary; and I'm afraid he did. And so we arrived in educated middle-class society feeling almost like spies, knowing that we had no social hinterland, that we had a great deal to conceal and a lot of pretending to do.

Interviewer: Did you feel ashamed of your father?
le Carré: I think that as I grew up I felt ashamed of myself, really. I could never quite understand why I had conformed with this vision he had of the way we should live—and I think that in that sense I always took myself to be something of a fraud.

It seems to me that story-telling comes partly from an urge to make an organised narrative out of chaos. I suppose that's why some of my novels attempt to make an arc through jungles of confusion. And I still feel, as I think Smiley does, that the components of life as we live it are irreconcilable, and chaotic. The art of survival is to function in spite of this.

Then again, because of my father, I've always been aware that there is only the narrowest membrane between the legal and the illegal, between the light side and the dark side of life. This has been very helpful to me in my writing—up to this point.

But I also feel at this moment in my career a great sense of relief that I have somehow paid a final tribute to that condition—that conspiratorial condition, if you will—and I feel free now, at last, to skate off in other directions and make the kind of literary experiments and literary mistakes which I was perhaps scared of making earlier.

Interviewer: What did your father think about your books?
le Carré: He didn't read them. He didn't like that kind of success. Not in his son. He even tried to sue me, after a television interview, for failing to give him the credit for my writing. It was funny, but very sad.

Interviewer: Tell me about your schooldays.
le Carré: I went to Sherborne, my brother to Radley. It was a very bad time for any public school because it was during the war. We were ruled by the rod, and by the athletes; we lived a cultureless existence in beautiful buildings, and we were heirs to preposterous prejudices. We were still being taught that the best career would take us to Rhodesia or Kenya, or that we should go

and rule India; and I think that even as a child I was overwhelmed by the arrogance of these assumptions.

I defected from Sherborne at the age of sixteen. I refused to go back and persuaded my father to send me to a foreign university, to Bern. I think my flight to Switzerland was in some ways almost that of a political refugee.

I was in Bern for a year. The Swiss are not naturally hospitable to penniless students and I had absolutely no money. I didn't really connect with anyone much, but I read a great deal. I learned German, and to some extent the local Swiss dialect, as a matter of survival, and that really launched me on my whole German connection. That was in 1948. I made my way to Germany, and to Berlin. Those who saw post-war Germany will never forget it. I think that was when I determined to study German in earnest.

I had a very long run of German: I studied German philosophy at Bern; I was posted to Austria in the Army; I read German at Oxford; I taught it at Eton, and I was posted into the German field in the Foreign Service.

Interviewer: You went into the Army after Bern?
le Carré: Yes, I did my military service with the British Army of occupation in Austria. I had an intelligence job which involved combing through "displaced persons" in the refugee camps. That was my first experience of people who were the victims of conflict—perennial prisoners and perennial refugees. I had two years in the Army, and for most of that time I was interrogating for various purposes.

Interviewer: And then you went to Oxford?
le Carré: I had difficulty getting in because I didn't have A-levels, but they took me and suddenly I began to learn things I should have learned at school. I was dreadfully ignorant and there are still frightful gaps in my general knowledge. Oxford was my salvation, and it was mainly brought about by the former Chaplain of Sherborne who became Senior Tutor at my College.

But in my second year my father's last major bankruptcy occurred with a great deal of publicity, and since in those days one didn't have grants and things—or at least I didn't—I had to go down with a lot of debts.

I taught for a year at Millfield, which at that time was a crammer for rich kids, and that taught me the terrors of trying to live a professional life without any qualifications. Then my father rallied a bit and produced some money, and my college very handsomely said that I could pay my fees later, so I went back.

Interviewer: Did you know anyone at Oxford, when you first went there?
le Carré: No, I found friends there, but haven't kept them. Perhaps writers keep growing up for too long. One's friends sit tight after a certain age. As a writer you can't afford to.

Interviewer: And after Oxford you taught at Eton?
le Carré: Yes, I really didn't know what to do when I was leaving Oxford and in the best British tradition I was talent-spotted for a job at Eton.

Interviewer: And were you ever talent-spotted for the Secret Service, like Smiley?
le Carré: No, but I've stopped beating my wife.[8] . . . And so I went to Eton. It was an absolutely fascinating time. I had never had any experience of the British ruling class before, and it probably coloured my later writing more than any other experience. People who rail against the English upper classes don't know how awful they really are—the way they talk, the way they function. Their prejudices are absolutely stunning.

At the time that I was there we had, I think, twelve or thirteen Old Etonians in the Cabinet. I was there during the Suez crisis, and I remember we got up a letter from young masters, which we sent to *The Times*, saying that we wished to dissociate ourselves from the actions of Old Etonians in the Cabinet.

Anthony Eden[9] was sufficiently furious that he found time to send down Lord John Hope, who I think was a Minister at the Foreign Office, in order to explain the rightness and necessity of the Suez action. I remember that those who were signatories to the letter got the most terrific rocket from the powers-that-be within the school.

But it was really the supposed misuse of our position that was most upsetting to the authorities—that we appeared to be speaking for Eton, and we were placing an unfair extra burden on the shoulders of an Old Etonian Prime Minister.

Interviewer: Do you think public schools should be abolished?
le Carré: Yes, they must. I feel thoroughly ashamed, as I think many people of my persuasion do, that I have been reduced to putting my four sons through

8. Old joke: "Have you stopped beating your wife? Answer yes or no." This is Cornwell's way of declining to answer the question.
9. British Prime Minister from 1955 to 1957.

the private educational system because it's there and because the state system is unreliable. You don't experiment with your own kith, but nevertheless I wish devoutly that we could get rid of public schools, and what I've seen of them only entrenches that wish.

Interviewer: How do you vote?
le Carré: I always vote Socialist—with misgivings. I would like to be able to vote Social Democrat. My father was a Liberal, of course, and stood for Parliament two or three times.

Interviewer: And why did you leave teaching for the Foreign Service?
le Carré: Well, it was just one of a series of involvements and escapes that have punctuated my life. I knew that teaching was not for me and I had, I suppose, in those days, a very ambitious nature and a very strong sense of frustration.

I hadn't started to write, and I felt that I had a creative side which had found no outlet. I did book illustrations and I tried to paint for a bit—I draw quite nicely but paint abominably. Bill Haydon had the same problem, I seem to remember. And then I thought perhaps I would find myself if I were more involved in administrative things, and more at the centre of life.

I spent most of my time in the Service in Germany, as second secretary in Bonn, and then as consul in Hamburg. And I did feel employed and active and at the centre of things, though I loathed the formalities and absurdities of diplomatic life. It was the time of the Berlin Wall, the Cuba crisis, the Adenauer-de Gaulle love affair, the end of the Adenauer government—a time of tremendous activity and tension. And you couldn't have been there at that period without being aware of the shadow of the enormous intelligence apparatus.

Interviewer: All the intelligence jargon that you bring into your books— "finding a legend," for instance—is it something you learned of at that time, or did you make it up?
le Carré: A "legend" is KGB jargon. It means a false biography, a cover story. "Mole" is also a KGB word which I flatter myself I dragged out of obscurity, but practically all the rest is invented—"the lamplighters," "the scalp-hunters" and so on—they are just much prettier names than the real ones.

Like all professions, of course, spies produce their own jargon and rather revel in it. And there is an eerie camaraderie between professional intelligence officers on different sides. Half the time they speak as though they were surgeons operating on the same body.

I thought it very important to give the reader the illusion of entering the secret world and to that end I invented a technical jargon that would be graphic and at the same time mysterious. Some people find it irritating—I rather like it.

Interviewer: You've told me why you went into the Foreign Service. Why did you leave it?

le Carré: For the same reason I left Eton, in a way. I didn't think it was for me. And meanwhile I'd written my first three books, in my spare time. With *The Spy Who Came in From the Cold* I reckoned that I was well enough off to take the risk of becoming a full-time writer.

I had given my accountant in London instructions that he should send me a cable when he thought I was worth, net, £20,000—an unattainable sum in those days. And when he sent me that cable, I handed in my resignation.

Interviewer: Why did you choose John le Carré as your pen-name?

le Carré: I don't know how it is these days, but in my day when someone in the Foreign Service wrote a book, even if it was about lepidoptera, it was the custom that he write under another name. So I went to Victor Gollancz, who was then my publisher, and he was all for a couple of strong monosyllables like "Chuck Smith." But I thought that to break up a name and give it a slightly foreign look would have the effect of printing it on people's memories.

I've told so many lies about where I got the name from, but I really don't remember. The one time I did the celebrity circuit in America, I was reduced to inventing the fiction that I'd been riding on a bus to the Foreign Office and abstracted the name from a shoe-shop. But that was simply because I couldn't convince anybody it came from nowhere.

Interviewer: You haven't quite convinced me, either. But anyway, is *Smiley's People* really the last of Smiley? You do leave open a slight possibility that he will return.

le Carré: I'm too old a dog to shove him over the Reichenbach Falls[10] but at the moment I can't imagine that he'll come back. On the other hand, I told myself the same thing before I started *Tinker, Tailor*, and indeed the first draft did not include Smiley at all. Then I became so despairing of getting in all the information, and I got so lost, that I was forced to get him out of mothballs.

One of the advantages of Smiley is his memory and the depth of his past. He is also very consoling to have around in a complex plot. When the reader feels lost, he at least believes that Smiley will always get him out of the maze. That was why Alec Guinness seemed so perfect for him: he had the same intellectual command which Smiley exerts over the plot.

Interviewer: Is there any truth in the rumour that Smiley is based on the former head of MI6, Sir Maurice Oldfield?
le Carré: No, there's none. I have said this repeatedly and it has made absolutely no difference: the Press believes what it wants to believe. When I first invented Smiley he was based to some extent on my mentor at Oxford—the man I spoke of—whom I admired very much; and partly on somebody I once worked with. But it was a very strange relationship I had with him because he was getting on for my father's age, and perhaps I was busy assembling some kind of substitute father—I've always had a rather filial relationship with Smiley.

Interviewer: What about Ann? Is it noble of him to go on loving her throughout all those years when she's consistently unfaithful, or is he supposed to be a bit foolish?
le Carré: Well, it's incompetent of him, of course. And yet it's the impossibility of love that is a romantic element in Smiley. In *Tinker, Tailor*, indeed I think in my last three Smiley books, she is that absent sexual force.

Interviewer: Who are the other writers who mean the most to you?
le Carré: Well, I was of course enormously influenced by Greene and I'm passionate about Conrad, and I love the big French story-tellers: I can read Balzac until I'm blue in the face.

---

10. Sir Arthur Conan Doyle attempted to end his Sherlock Holmes stories by having the hero killed at the Reichenbach Falls; but Doyle was compelled by reader demand to resuscitate Holmes.

They're not all heavies though—P. G. Wodehouse for rhythm and timing; Conan Doyle for thrust and instant atmosphere. Then back to the Germans for their moral search. . . . I think the strongest literary influence was all that German literature that I devoured either compulsorily or voluntarily, and Balzac appealed to me from the start because he's so good on the dark side, on the fusion of the legal and the illegal.

The other literary influence, I suppose, is Foreign Office drafting: the discipline of submitting draft after draft which goes all the way up to the Ambassador, through all the different echelons in an embassy, and then all the way down again. Then you rewrite and rewrite; and the Foreign Office also teaches a great sense of responsibility about what you put on paper.

Everything has to be honed and considered. With Foreign Office cables, at least in my day, it was obligatory to put on the telegram how much it had cost to send. And that taught one to be pretty fussy with words.

As for my own writing, the real fun is the fun of finding that you've enchanted people—enchanted them in the sense that you've admitted them to a world they didn't know about.

The Little Drummer Girl: An Interview with John le Carré

Melvyn Bragg / 1983

Reprinted from *The Quest for le Carré* (London: Vision Press, 1988; New York: St. Martin's Press, 1988), pp. 129–43. *South Bank Show* (27 March 1983). Copyright © South Bank Television. Reprinted by permission.

Before discussing The Little Drummer Girl *in detail with the author, Melvyn Bragg raised an issue that has fascinated readers of le Carré. Bragg observed that various commentators assumed that, while working for the Foreign Office, le Carré "acted as a spy," in which capacity he encountered situations subsequently used in his novels. Le Carré's answer is the closest he has come to settling the issue:*

le Carré: Well, to an extent, it's true. I wasn't Mata Hari, and I wasn't Himmler's Aunt, but it would be stupid of me to pretend that I was not—like Somerset Maugham, Graham Greene and lots of other writers—for a time engaged in that work. And it was a natural continuum, really, of the life I had led. . . . I've always tried to deny it, and keep away from the subject, and I intend to go on doing so. Firstly, because I simply don't want to commit a breach of confidence; and secondly, because it seems to me really to belong— it's so long ago—to an extension of my childhood, rather than adulthood. I loathe the notion that I'm some kind of literary defector from the secret world. That's really all I want to say about it.

Interviewer: *The Little Drummer Girl* is set all over Europe but centred very heavily in the Middle East. And it's a non-Smiley book. Can you say why you wanted the Middle East as a subject first of all?
le Carré: Well, my interest in the Middle East began after I'd written *The Honourable Schoolboy*, when I still had it in mind to take Smiley around the world and have him fighting it out with Karla, his Russian opposite number, in different theatres. So in 1978 I went to the Lebanon and to Israel and I tried to familiarize myself with the area and its problems. I simply could not find a plot which was not too Gothic, too manipulative—too silly really—to

accommodate that conflict. The Soviet presence in the Middle East, at that time, was very slight indeed, I mean the Russians have goofed in the Middle East anyway and they were effectively thrown out of Egypt. I just couldn't find a point at which to come in with the story so I put it aside and wrote *Smiley's People* instead and then, when Smiley was tucked away, I thought I would go back without all that luggage of the Circus and some great British conspiracy, Russian conspiracy; all of that was swept aside and I just went and goofed around again. I went to Israel and then back to the Lebanon and stayed in Beirut and I went down to the Palestinian camps at Rashovdiyeh and Nabatiyeh, the camp in Sidon itself, explored the camps in Beirut, and out of that began to make quite a different story which drew upon totally different elements. I wanted also to write about much younger people than were given to me by the Smiley world, I also wanted to write more about women. So I took as my central character—through whom we perceived the Middle East and the Middle Eastern problem—an English girl, an actress. Actors and actresses were very much in mind too because of mucking around with actors and actresses over the two B.B.C. dramatizations, *Tinker Tailor* and *Smiley's People* and I have also a very beautiful sister, Charlotte,[1] who is an actress and whose life was, in crude terms, the raw material that got me off the ground. Those were the things that came together.

Interviewer: As you say, *The Little Drummer Girl* is about an English actress who is used by Israeli intelligence to penetrate Palestinian intelligence.
le Carré: Not Palestinian intelligence, but a breakaway Palestinian group that is conducting anti-Jewish operations around Europe.

Interviewer: An English actress is used by Israeli intelligence to get to an extremely successful Palestinian guerrilla group.
le Carré: Yes, that's right.

Interviewer: Like a lot of your novels it has an enormous number of layers in it. It reads as if you've done an immense amount of ground research in the Middle East. Can you give us some idea of the sort of research you did?
le Carré: I began with Israel because Israel is much more accessible. The Israelis help. They invited me, allowed me to see anybody I wanted to see. In

---

1. Charlotte Cornwell, le Carré's half sister, has been a actress on the British stage more than thirty years.

many ways it's an extraordinarily open society. If you want to see General so-
and-so, somebody calls him up, you get an introduction to go along, he gives
you time. I wanted to meet chaps from the Israeli and Special Forces. People
who'd been in secret outfits. The Israelis enabled me to go and talk to their
Palestinian prisoners, they even allowed me to talk to a German girl they
were holding in prison, who had been allegedly involved in a Palestinian terror operation in Kenya. Otherwise in Israel: moving, talking, thinking,
spending time with people, just going where the wind blew. The Palestinians
were a much more difficult nut to crack, in a way, because they have no
Public Relations worth talking of—they speak very poorly for themselves, in
my opinion, and you go so far and then somehow you get no further. But I
did eventually manage to find the right connections and, through them, I was
received by Yassir Arafat in Beirut and had one of those celebrated nocturnal
conversations with him. He said, "Please, why have you come to me, what do
you want?" And I said, "Well, Mr. Chairman, I'm trying to put my hand on
the Palestinian heart." And he grasped my hand and held it to his own breast
and said, "Sir, it is here, it is here." I found him very interesting, very touch-
ing, very genuine and I don't think I'm as starry-eyed as I might appear. I did
think he was a much maligned man by comparison with most of the people
in his outfit. He's extremely moderate and, indeed, if we are to see his
downfall—which is quite possible—it will be because of his moderation. He
said, "What are you going to do tomorrow night?" which was New Year's Eve,
and I said I had no plans and he said, "Well, come up to the school for the
martyrs," and so again I hung around in my hotel. Eventually cars came and
we were whisked from one side of Beirut to the other, changed cars—it was
all very exciting—and we got into a convoy and roared up the hill outside
Beirut, up this snake hill in pouring rain behind a red Landrover. We shot
through Syrian checkpoints, everybody's checkpoints, and finished at the
school and we all leaped out of the car and went to greet the occupant of the
red Landrover. The doors opened and out got a couple of boys I didn't recognize. Arafat was already at the school, he takes care of his personal security
very well. So we sat in the audience at this packed school of orphans, children
of people who have died fighting for Palestine. And the kids, on the stage,
staged a Palestinian dance, and they were tossing wooden rifles back and
forth. The dance has a very emphatic rhythm and the audience began doing
this. . . . Suddenly Arafat, just down the row from me, put out his arms like
this and two of his fighting men seized him and tossed him up onto the

stage. He took the back of this *kaffiyeh* and began, to this hypnotic rhythm, leading this kind of weird congo round the stage. When it was over, and everybody by then was clapping and urging him on, he came to the edge of the stage and again spread out his arms and leapt straight into the air, straight off the edge of the podium and his boys caught him and put him back in his seat. He's a very infectious man; tremendously spontaneous and very witty and it's said Beirut is still full of stories about him, one of them being that when they came to him and said, "Look, the seige is over, the deal is done and the Lebanese want to come and say goodbye," Arafat said, "Why, where are they going?" That was Arafat. I saw him a couple of times more, it was really only from a distance and through him and through his staff I was able to go down to the camps.

Interviewer: The contact with Arafat gave you introductions to other areas.
le Carré: Yes. Then I went south and things were extremely tense because by then everybody knew that it was only a matter of time before the Israelis would come, and it was just spoken of as an inevitable fact that the big invasion would come. As the Palestinians put it, they were going to try and wipe us out, it was no secret anywhere. I stayed again, not through Arafat but through other connections, in a house in Sidon which belonged to a Palestinian commander of troops. He had a lot of fighting kids around the house and some not-fighting kids, just students and people. I talked a lot to them and there was one who carried no gun and was a very studious-looking chap and hardly ever spoke, and I thought he must be the spook and made every kind of attempt to get alongside him. I asked him questions and always received very bland replies, and then we all went down to Sidon to watch the procession to celebrate the Palestinian revolution. Most of the kids who were looking after me or looking after the house were in the procession, but this boy was not, so I said to him, "Why were you not in the procession?" and he said, "Please, I have night work." I said, "What is your night work?" He said, "Special work." I said, "What do you do at night?" He said, "You notice the boy scouts, the little boys in the procession, they wear on their breast a photograph of our Chairman Arafat." I said yes, I had noticed. He said, "I personally, all through the night, work with a hot iron on the photographs." So I realized that perhaps he wasn't a spy. And I talked to people in the camps and got the feel of it, and became astonished really with one very simple perception that seems to me to have made no headway in the West at all: that one

can, indeed as I am, be greatly in favour of the state of Israel and wish for its survival but that in the making of Israel a great crime was committed, not numerically commensurate with the crime that was committed against the Jews, but appalling all the same. Millions of people displaced, others subjugated with total alien types of rules, turned into second-class citizens. The image of the Palestinians, largely invented, as crazies carrying guns and so on was so far removed from the reality of the majority of the Palestinian people that it needed saying, it needed demonstrating—and not by some maverick Trotskyist, or something, but by somebody like myself who has written extensively, with great passion I like to think, about Jews in the past but found in this situation an injustice which needs reporting.

Interviewer: So that was one of the spurs of the book.
le Carré: Yes. Like my character Charlie, I had a love affair with the Palestinians, exactly as in the past I've had a love affair with the Jews. It is my job to radicalize, my job to feel that way.

Interviewer: So you have the ground out there, the revelation is the Palestinian problem, because the Israeli problem we know a lot about, it's well reported. The Palestinian situation is new territory, both in fact and in the perception it gives you of the fact.
le Carré: And in popular fiction. I mean we've all had *Exodus* until it comes out of our ears. We all have that image of Israel in different forms but, as it happens, I don't think anybody's written with anything like compassion about the Palestinians.

Interviewer: So you go there, you want to radicalize and report. Now the other big element coming in is an English actress who is somehow going to come together with this material. Can you give us some fix on why it was an English actress, where she came from and how you wanted to weld her to this material?
le Carré: It didn't have to be an English actress, it had to be a Western one. Charlie is, in my book, about twenty-eight. She's a person of extremely strong conscience, she wishes for a moral anchor, she wishes for a discipline, if you will. But although she's rejecting, she really wants to join—a feeling that I know about—and what the Israelis offer her is all the things which I believe actresses, or for that matter women of that age, would fall for: a direction, a

purpose, a mission, the family attachment; the mind control, if you like, which tells her what to think and who to be. She has loyalty in her pocket like loose change and they show her how to spend it, how to invest it, who to be. Now I'm not suggesting that every woman can be manipulated in such a way but there are people who have a surge towards an absolute, in the same way that, for instance, Patti Hearst was turned from (one assumes) a spoilt little millionairess into a radical fighter. It seems impossible, it seems terribly hard to write, but we accept it in real life. Charlie, when she's first picked up by the Israelis, is loosely radical, pro-Palestinian. They don't discount that in the least; they like that part of her but they take hold of her and they control her and they recruit her and they turn her into a double agent. In that sense it's an exploration of the double agent which I began in *Tinker, Tailor*.

Interviewer: And it's also an exploration or a continuation of the idea of fiction working itself out in real life which is one of the things your books are about. Which is to say, that Charlie's also given a rôle.
le Carré: Yes, that's right, a job, for an actress above all; a part, as they put it to her, in the theatre of the real, that as an actress you must always have had that appetite to experience real life; to play a part in real life, you must have felt the confinement of theatre: now join us and you can continue to act but it's the theatre of the real and you'll be doing good and we love you, all of us we love you.

Interviewer: You have the circumstances that you found in the Middle East and you want to declare or bear witness to these. You have the actress and you've mentioned your sister and being involved with actors and actresses in the productions of *Tinker, Tailor* and *Smiley's People*. But with a book, a lot of its power has got to come from authenticity. Did you go back and check that it was at all plausible for an English Shakespearean actress to be recruited by Israeli intelligence for such an important job?
le Carré: Well, I put it to the lads in Israel and they were enchanted with the idea and said: yes if it would work, yes they would do it. You see Israel, from an intelligence point of view, is the sandbox—you can do anything as long as it works. They see themselves as totally surrounded by hostile forces. Security is survival. If they lose a battle, they've already lost the war. If they lose the war, they've lost Israel. That's how they feel, and so the intelligence arm is an absolutely crucial one and the intelligence world in Israel is to be found

everywhere. Dons get into it and come out of it the moment a war starts or a crisis appears; people put down their academic books and flood to secret offices around the place. They have a highly developed intelligence service and above all a highly motivated one and, of course, because it's a well-kept secret, I don't know how the devolution of power works. I don't know what freedoms the Mossad has or the Israeli security service has, but I suspect, however much they would deny it, that they're far greater than are available to the C.I.A. or to our own.

Interviewer: *The Little Drummer Girl* is about a great number of things, but the main line of the story is that an English actress is picked up by Israeli intelligence, turned into a double agent and sent on a mission to destroy a particularly effective group of Palestinian guerrillas. Now the fact that your sister, Charlotte, is an English actress and a redhead and that she was acting in the West Country, where we meet the Charlie in the book, is obviously relevant.
le Carré: Yes. There is a scene in the book which is set in the West Country, where Charlie is on tour with an unnamed travelling company, and in fact my sister was travelling with the Royal Shakespeare Company and performing at Camborne at the Sports Centre there. I was here alone and I went up to see her and it was pouring with rain, the most unbelievable noise on the roof, and Charlotte was really having to belt it out. I thought she was very good but she was over the top. I mean she was booming in order to defeat the rain and it was actually the moment, I think, where I thought: yes, I'll use that. I'll have Charlotte for my character, at least this, and I kept the episode. It's absurd to say that it is my sister, but for most characters there is a point of departure and that was hers. It was that night really, that I brought her back here with a couple of kids from the touring company and we spent a pleasantly drunken night here, that the plot began to shape up.

Interviewer: As you'd researched the Middle East, did you research the actress background? Let's leave your sister Charlotte to one side, but Charlie, in the book, is an actress figure who has been to a "radicalizing" school in England and been taught about revolution and is a left-wing type of actress—of whom there are several in this country—who believes very passionately in extreme measures. Did that need finding out about?
le Carré: I sort of knew about it really. Not to bring Charlotte up again, but it was, in fact, her experience also. She did go to one of those places. She went

through a dotty time politically and emerged from it very fast, and she talked to me a bit about it. And I went up to Islington and mucked around various funny bookshops there that feed the extreme left, and the radical causes, and talked to one or two people in that world.

Interviewer: Where did you decide that the book's perception should lie? You had two lots of material—the Middle East aspect and the actress side—and a desire to witness and depict a radical idea. Having got the mechanism of the intelligence service, you then have the point of view. Now what point of view did you decide on, and why?

le Carré: I settled for the irreconcilability of the problem. I mined, first, my own feelings about it which are, very simply, that there is a terrible historical irony in the fact that because—very properly and far too late—the Jews engaged our western conscience, we gave them a country which was not ours to give. And we in fact obliged the Palestinians to pay the price for the western conscience. It was not the Palestinians who persecuted the Jews, it was us. Us westerners. It was us Brits for not letting them in, it was the Americans for not letting them in, it was a whole mucky western conspiracy of which the Germans were the spearhead, but we are not without blame in the matter. That, on the one hand; then, on the other, the lamentable fact that in the protection of Israeli security Israel, in my opinion, has gone overboard, particularly under this government. I don't think it is allowable simply because the Jews have been persecuted that Mr. Begin can draw his own borders and turf out more people or subjugate them. That seems to me to be a modern monstrosity. So, one's conscience was doubly engaged. Beyond that I was determined to balance the story as perfectly as I knew how and so the point of view became Charlie's, it became the ambivalent perception. The capacity to fall in love, the twice-promised girl, and I don't think that there are any opinions expressed which do not actually proceed from characters because I knew this was going to be an egg-walk. As the Germans say, I would be dancing on eggshells and a lot of people would be very cross. The great heresy is not that I have said anything unpleasant about the Israelis, but that I have actually raised the Palestinians to the point where their claim is made clear. I think that that—particularly in the United States—is liable to upset a great number of people and I don't think it's been done before.

Interviewer: Going through another layer, *The Little Drummer Girl* links up with *The Naïve and Sentimental Lover* in that the fulcrum of the whole thing is an idea of a commitment to a particular personal love affair. From my reading of the book, when Charlie, recruited by Israeli intelligence, falls in love with this man, Joseph, and goes to do her job behind Palestinian lines, she has, naturally, perceptions about Palestine which you've been describing yourself and is then totally torn and her loyalties given in the end to this particular man, Joseph.

le Carré: Whose loyalties, of course, are ambiguous. As a fighting Israeli who has given the whole of his youth to the various wars, he feels now that the things he fought for are not there.

Interviewer: Did you find that hard to write, in the sense that all writing is to do with committing yourself first? That this would be, that her commitment to him could be so strong, that it could survive her education and radicalization and realizations in Palestine, in the Palestinian area?

le Carré: I found it difficult to write. I found Joseph altogether—the character of her Israeli agent runner—the most difficult to deal with. For technical reasons, because we had to experience him in the first instance through her, I could not cut away into Joseph's own mind because to do so would destroy the mystery of who he was, which was kindled in Charlie.

Interviewer: In the end you have got to believe as a writer, and we believe as readers, that for love of this man, Joseph, Charlie will in a sense deny the amazing and shocking experience of what she discovers behind the Palestinian lines. You're actually testing the strength of your own story. It's a mixture of loyalty, responsibility and credibility that you're looking for in Charlie, as a reader and as a writer.

le Carré: That's right. The linch-pin is her relationship with her agent runner, her controller. I think there is, there must be, something quite extraordinary in the relationship between male agent runner and female agent: a kind of Pygmalion relationship. He's the link man, he speaks for the organization for her, he gives her a personal gloss, to her brief, he debriefs her, he must man-manage her emotions. He is the manipulator, he is the giver of love and the receiver of love. If that relationship doesn't work, no other relationship works. Therefore for Charlie, to be in love with him is almost a masochistic necessity of the operation for her, and the moment when she ceases to love him, she's done something perfectly dreadful. She's committed a betrayal on an unforgettable scale. Indeed, by the end of the story, she knows she's done that anyway, but Joseph holds her to the line until then, which is his job.

Interviewer: But it's really two sorts of betrayal facing each other, because by betraying the Palestinians she gets a lot of people—who we come to like very much—killed. She holds to that but destroys that. There is a good deal of bleakness, unlike the Smiley novels where there's always Smiley, a good man. I mean, it's very bleak.

le Carré: There is no consolation, Smiley isn't there to cheer us up and explain things and say we'll carry on another time. When the curtain comes down, as Charlie is warned in the theatre of the real, nobody gets up and goes home. The bodies stay where they are. She learns that, so the end, I imagine, is bleak and ambiguous. But the feel of love betrayed has really gone on, I think, in most of the books all the way through. In *Tinker, Tailor* love is abused, misused: the baddie had slept with Smiley's wife in order to put Smiley off the scent. People manipulate one another in so many of the books, by means of love, that I don't think it is out of line in that respect.

Interviewer: No. There has always been the contrast between private and public morality. Is the reason you acclaim private morality because at least you might know the consequences of it?

le Carré: At least you know what your feelings are. When you accept a larger institutional argument, of the sort Charlie accepted, there are complications: when they are recruiting her she asks who do we kill and the reply is—only somebody who has entirely broken the human bond. Who has lost our claim to compassion, him we must kill, say the Israelis. And she says, who are you to say that has happened? And their answer is glossed over. What was the first bond that was broken, who cast the first stone? God alone knows. So the institutional conflict cannot be resolved in the story and personal love suffers, is adjusted accordingly.

Interviewer: We've been talking about some of the themes and the areas of material you've drawn on in this novel. Driving it through is a very tightly planned plot which is unravelled, checked back on: go in this direction, go in that direction, so it fools you. It's plotted in enormous detail, and at some length. What do you think the value of that is, to take it in so much detail, to plot it so ingeniously? What value do you give to that, as a writer?

le Carré: It gives a monstrous logic to the manipulation of Charlie, I think. With a story of this kind the whole premise is that they take a girl like that and manipulate her life from beginning to end, so that we are constantly dealing with the taming of Charlie, the breaking in of Charlie, the winning of Charlie. To spread around her all the evidence of meticulous planning is actually to remind the reader all the time that they are doing that to Charlie as well, that there is no part of her life, no corner of her character that they have not taken into account, not examined, not studied, put into the scales before they recruited her, and while they are running her.

Interviewer: That's one sort of value I can see you get from this sort of plotting. What value does it give your characters? Do you feel it gives them more room to breathe, gives them things to work against?
le Carré: Well, Charlie's pulling all the time at the bridle. So I think that it gives a dramatic tension. It also, in pompous terms, gives them a relationship. The destiny that is being woven around Charlie is one which, in a sense, she wished upon herself. She is a girl whose bluff was called. But all the posturing and attitudes and all the lies she's told, all the little cheating that she's got up to, all of these things are now put into effect. Very well, if you are that kind of person, be it, but more so; be it in extension and put all your sins and all your virtues to our service. It's a very beguiling guide, it's a crusade, a mission, which takes up all the slack in this wayward, rather gooky, character.

Interviewer: Would you say *The Little Drummer Girl* was, in any structural way, a departure from your earlier novels?
le Carré: I think it's a far more passionate book, probably the most passionate. It's the maddest. I think that within Charlie, within that controlled schizophrenia, there are scenes which, when you start taking them apart, are at the very edge of sanity. I found that very hard to write, and it's a very hard book for me to get out of mentally. Beyond that I think I would have to leave the answer to the critics. I don't know. I think it's the same as the other books, but more so, and of course the sexuality is much greater. It takes on things that I couldn't take on in the earlier books because of the characters I used, and perhaps, in some ways, because of my own nature. It's just the way I've changed.

Interviewer: To come back to one of the starting points of the book, when you went to the Middle East you discovered the Palestinian cause which radicalized your thinking. Do you think your book represents and bears witness to the strength of feeling you had then, and do you think the work of fiction can do anything about it?

le Carré: I am necessarily limited by a considerable concern for Israel, also. It's enough, I think, to do what I've done. I think that, with any luck, I would have opened people's minds much more to the reality of the Palestinian tragedy without going overboard and, if I've done that, nobody but the most bigoted Israeli or Jew would attack me for it. I'm not afraid of that attack, but I'm very afraid of the book being characterized as anti-Israeli which is really, coming out of modern Israel, almost a cheap jibe. It drives me absolutely mad. A great number of books, some of them pulp, have almost blindly extolled the making of Israel and neglected entirely the Palestinian matter. Golda Meir, as you probably know, said the Palestinians did not exist; there was a slogan, a land without people for a people without land. Now these things were not fair and not just. I think that in terms of popular fiction, simply by putting a human face upon the Palestinians by revealing the human tragedy, it's enough. It's enough thus far. I haven't gone nearly as far in the book, for instance, as the Israeli left would go within Israel, but then I'm a gentile. There are other things I regret very much, which I can't control. One of them is the premise in the book that Beirut, around the time when the story occurred, was still the capital of terrorism which could be taken as a justification for the Israeli invasion of the Lebanon in 1982. It is a fact, of which I only recently became aware, that the Palestinians moved all their operational centres away from Beirut at the beginning of the cease-fire, so I would have written that differently too. But, by and large, the book does a job. I have reacted much more vehemently in the press at the time of the Israeli invasion. I did write a piece ["Memories of a Vanished Land"] in the *Observer* [13 June 1982] which attracted a great deal of flack, and so on, but when it comes to actually drawing the balance, it's almost enough to have corrected the cliché which required everybody to say piously "I believe in the survival of Israel." They forgot that they also believed, if they were even aware of it, in the survival of the Palestinians. So that's enough.

Interviewer: There are those who would say that Arafat has committed acts of terrorism and so have the Palestinians and that, in a sense, by meeting him and—to a certain extent—taking his side, you are committing yourself to that aspect of life as well. What would you say to that?

le Carré: I would say that it was nonsense. To talk to him, to try and understand him, is already the right thing to do whatever he's done, but I can't think, offhand, of many heads of states, or heads of organizations in that part of the world, with whom one could sit down with a clear conscience. I wouldn't really want to sit with Kissinger after the bombing of Cambodia. I don't think I would have been allowed to have sat with Jomo Kenyata, after his association with the Mau Mau. I would certainly feel a bit queezy about sitting next to Begin after the invasion of the Lebanon. The fact of the matter is, by exploring the roots of Palestinian anger one gets closer to understanding the acts of violence. Also, I do not know what terror is. I mean, is it an act of terror to send Israeli aeroplanes over a camp, to drop a cluster bomb, kill two or three hundred people, or is terror already legitimized by the fact that you have an air force?

If you are a displaced people, and you've got to make the world listen, that is the Palestinian argument. If you've been driven from camp to camp, if you've had the living daylight persecuted out of you by your own people—by the Israelis but above all by your brother Arabs—I can understand that you would turn to violence. And very many people who have this cliché vision of the Palestinians would themselves, if they had been subjected to the same harassment and persecution and humiliation, if they had no passport, no friends, no permanent home, if they'd been bombed out of one place after another all through their lives, from the age of practically nothing—many of those people would have taken the violent path. I think the amazing thing is, how little has actually happened on the Palestinian side. I think it's outrageous that the Israelis simply refer to the Palestinians now as terrorists. That really is a piece of propaganda overkill which I think will bounce back in time. In the second month of the Israeli invasion of the Lebanon, the Israelis killed more children than have died in all the Palestinian operations against Israel. So I don't know what terrorism means in this category. I certainly loathe, as we all do, these wanton acts against civilian people. They are appalling and unthinkable, and that is part of the awfulness of my story. But I really would not think of Arafat as having exceptionally bloody hands.

Interviewer: In the fiction, in *The Little Drummer Girl,* what are you saying about Charlie's relationship with terrorism? What, in your opinion, justifies her in it?

le Carré: They tell her specifically that she will save innocent life and, indeed, it is true, it's absolutely true, she prevents a maverick Palestinian bomber from bombing any more; in that sense she does right. But in the course of doing right she understands the roots of his anger, and she understands how he turned the corner and took the violent path. But there's absolutely no sense, anywhere in the book, of anybody condoning it, let alone myself doing that.

Interviewer: Finally, then, could I come back to the idea of fiction? The book has references to the theatre of the real and the idea of people perceiving things in terms of inventions, that being the way they tackle things that are mysterious to them, that are unpalatable to them. That is also what you have done about this situation in the Middle East. What do you think are the consolations and benefits that come from that?
le Carré: To whom? To me?

Interviewer: Yes. As a writer of this particular novel.
le Carré: I think I have externalized things in my own past about which I was intensely uncomfortable: forms of artificial behaviour if you like, a sense of dislocation between personal behaviour and internal reality. I think that by making the story function in so many different theatrical stages of the same stage I've maybe, in some quite therapeutic way, cut through personal deceptions to some sort of centre. I think that that is nothing new for any writer. Most of us are fairly weak creatures in one way or another; it's absurd to appoint us as great gurus but, after all, our job is to combine perception with internal fantasy and to spin out of it something which produces a new reality for other people and gives a narrative.

Interviewer: And it's the story, finally, that carries the message of your idea of realities? By discovering the story the whole business makes sense for you and therefore, you hope, for someone else?
le Carré: Yes. And to entertain, to stimulate, to cause to ponder, to excite, to stretch and to have that sense of company that people feel with you, any entertainer. As a comedian tries to fight off ridicule, so perhaps a thriller writer tries to cauterize tension or reconcile components within himself by setting them out in different characters. In the end it should be a story.

Spying on a Spymaker

Pierre Assouline / 1986

Reprinted from *World Press Review*, 33 (August 1986), pp. 59–60. *Lire*, Summer 1986. Reprinted by permission of Pierre Assouline.

Interviewer: How might you review your latest book, *A Perfect Spy*?

le Carré: It is the book of a lifetime. If you dislike John le Carré's work, you will dislike this book especially. But if you like le Carré, you will be glad he has written this book, his most radical and subversive, a book in which he overturns accepted ideas.

My hero, Pym, works for both the Communists and the West—and he nearly loses his head. He is the archetype of the double agent in all of us. We live much of our lives beneath the surface—like icebergs. Most of our thoughts and desires are unexpressed.

Interviewer: How long did you take to write it?

le Carré: I had this novel in mind for a long time—even before I began writing my first book. Over the years, I have tried to write it, but in vain. Each time I tried I thought it was the book of my life and that I would never write it, so I wrote others that revolved around it. Despite their success, I could not detach myself from this project. It was like a mountain that I could not scale. I was especially frustrated because the literature treating father-son relationships left me dissatisfied.

I finally realized that I would not be able to write about my father until I was able to balance our respective guilt and responsibility. The problem was in not assigning too much to one who would automatically win the reader's sympathy. As long as my pen produced a virtuous son and a monstrous father, my story was not right—any more than when my sympathy was for the father trying to raise a conceited little monster. I did not begin to enjoy it until I introduced a criminal tendency in the boy, removing all moral sense from him while leaving him a conscience. The novel became a sort of catharsis. I exorcized my father.

Naturally, some readers will try to ascertain what is real and what is fictitious in this. I leave that to them. The responsibility of the writer is to observe, listen and record. Then he tells a story, adding imagination to experience, and it bares the scars of his soul.

Interviewer: What was your father like?

le Carré: He lived extravagantly, running up big bills at the best restaurants and leaving unpaid hotel bills in Venice or Zürich. He was a man who spent without restraint, who involved himself in all sorts of deals, who owned horses and threw big parties when he did not have a cent. Several times he filed fraudulent bankruptcies, which did not prevent him from starting new companies—each as wasteful as the others.

He was a financial adventurer. He served time in prison. He died at sixty-nine from a heart attack in 1975. He claimed not to have read a book in his life, not mine or anyone else's.

He led, at the least, a double life. He was a secretive man who forced my brother and me to spy on him in order to know him. In the absence of our mother, who left us early on, he gave us first-rate educations so that we would succeed where he had failed: to be respected and respectable.

My father's lifestyle was vulgar, nouveau riche and immoral according to conventional criteria. When he took off for long trips, my brother and I were exposed to highly unorthodox situations. We had to give the appearance of living another kind of life. That forced us to cultivate our imaginations.

But he used us for his schemes. Once he sent us to Paris to retrieve his golf clubs from the George V hotel—without telling us that he had left them as security against an unpaid bill.

Once, learning that I had not mentioned him in an interview in which I had recounted my life, he wanted to sue me. He loved a tribunal. In the end, he struck a compromise with my lawyer: compensation of $14,000. Nonetheless, I have given him minor roles in some of my novels.

I probably took refuge in the world of espionage to escape my father. By inventing George Smiley I tried to conjure up the specter of my father. To understand, explain and justify my father's betrayal of his milieu, class and society, one has to blame the institutions and the men behind them as well as the respectability in which I found temporary refuge when I fled.

Interviewer: Do you read spy novels?

le Carré: Never. I like Joseph Conrad very much. I recently reread Graham Greene's *Our Man in Havana*, which is truly fantastic, and not long ago

I enjoyed reading his *The Quiet American* when I was in Vietnam. But it is not for reasons of snobbery that I do not read others' spy novels. I have my secret world and it is nourished not by books but by life—the world at large.

When time permits I read contemporary novels that have nothing to do with espionage—such as *The Lover* by Marguerite Duras, or something by Françoise Sagan or García Márquez. I have read the investigative reporting of William Shawcross on Cambodia. I try to keep up with what is new.

Interviewer: They say you are influenced by Balzac and Dickens.
le Carré: I adore Dickens. Philosophers and bureaucrats always have taught us that childhood is a period and a category, whereas Dickens knew that childhood is life itself. I have been influenced by Dickens, but only to a point. He never took the risk of making his principal character a scoundrel.

Balzac's extraordinary technique was to begin novels with a detail of no consequence—the slippers of the priest of Tours, for instance. Balzac was a great storyteller, as hard-hitting in his description of the church as of the salons, the middle class, the bourgeoisie and especially hypocrisy. I envy this apparent ability to speak from the center of life. He wrote like someone born in the middle of the human race.

Interviewer: Are you, like George Smiley, a "failed intellectual"?
le Carré: Certainly. The intellectual life bores me enormously. At Oxford I did everything necessary to obtain the right diplomas so I could become a researcher or don, but I was too curious to be satisfied with university life. Besides, I like writing and telling a story.

Interviewer: How do you write?
le Carré: According to simple principles. Like a professional athlete, I devote to writing the best hours of my day: early in the morning. I wrote the last six chapters of *A Perfect Spy* between 4 a.m. and 10 a.m., before the rest of the world had awakened. It is a habit I formed when I was a diplomat. The embassies rarely open before 10 a.m. You can thus gain half a day of work.

I always write by hand. I cannot type; I cannot find the letters on the keyboard. I like the rhythm of a written manuscript, the pen and paper. When you alter something it is instantaneous. There is something purely physical in this process of artistic creation. When one writes slowly one self-censors, and with a glance one can see the archeology of the manuscript.

Interviewer: Where do you work?
le Carré: If I had to begin a book in the months to come, which I hope to do, I would start writing in London. So that I may work without disturbance, I have a room in that city whose whereabouts I keep secret. After a few weeks, if the book is off to a good start and I have a good sense of how it will develop, I take the night train to my house in Cornwall.

Interviewer: How do ideas come to you?
le Carré: In the beginning I have a character, a marriage, a woman, a conflict, a cat sitting in a man's lap, a cinematic opening scene, a way of going back into the past, one or two key scenes. I know the end of the story and I know how I am going to get there. If I do not put these ideas on paper, I will spend five or six weeks on the first two pages.

Interviewer: Some readers consider your plots too complicated.
le Carré: I do not agree. The people who offer that complaint are not prepared to make any intellectual effort. My books generally have two principal characters and a crowd of minor characters, as in life. I am convinced that the reader likes to work a little and at the end is happy to have resolved a somewhat complex story.

Interviewer: Do you have any political opinions?
le Carré: All I desire is that humane values be maintained in our institutions, codes of conduct and systems of thought. It is probably nothing more than old-fashioned liberalism.

Interviewer: What do you believe in?
le Carré: My books can be defined first by what I do not believe in: constancy, group values, obligations. I see in what I write a constant progress toward individual values and an anger that is growing more intense toward injustice.

John le Carré on Perfect Spies and Other Characters

Thom Schwarz / 1987

Reprinted from *Writer's Digest*, 67 (February 1987), pp. 20–21. Copyright © *Writer's Digest*. Reprinted by permission.

David John Moore Cornwell—the former British Foreign Service agent who writes as John le Carré—recently talked with New York freelancer Thom Schwarz about crafting characters in general, and his main spy George Smiley in particular.

Interviewer: How much of your own experiences as a spy do you draw upon to use in your novels?

le Carré: A lot of the early cases I gave to Smiley were the frustrations of a desk man. I never felt the wind of a bullet pass my cheek, I assure you. I've been in two wars, but only to put a toe in the water: Cambodia and Vietnam for *The Honourable Schoolboy* and then for *The Little Drummer Girl* I got on the wrong end of one or two situations in Beirut. Nothing that would be outside the ordinary afternoon of one correspondent.

Interviewer: When you craft character, you take parts from people you meet and parts from yourself. Some characters seem to be grafted together. Do you ever lift someone straight out of life onto the pages of your books?

le Carré: I don't think there has ever been a time when I have stolen one person lock, stock and barrel: I wouldn't know enough about him. When you have done all your thieving and put your character together, you've got to fill him with your own breath. That's what makes the character play. It isn't that he talks like dear old so-and-so who lives up the road. It's that you speak through him and give him life, which is the narcissistic part of writing. When you really hear the right voice speaking through him, you know you have another fragment of yourself moving through the book.

Interviewer: Isn't there a lot of you in Smiley?

le Carré: He was twenty-five years older than I am, but we had a lot of the same characteristics, as well as sharing a lot of experiences in Middle Europe just after World War II. We'd both seen the ghosts in the rubble, if you will; knew what the true cost of war was. We'd both been witnesses to the seamless transition from the hot to the cold war, and the almost unconscious realignment of political alliances. We'd both seen a world where American kids bombed Berlin in 1945 and ran the Berlin airlift in 1948. The concept of the Good German was hastily developed, and that was the German who didn't like Communists, and we'd sort of forgotten that the first inmates of the concentration camps were Communists. Those Orwellian ideologic leaps from quite early in my own life left scars, and I put them on Smiley's soul rather than my own.

I had a very mucky childhood in the shadow of a very volatile but flawed businessman who was in and out of prison. So I made Smiley a guy with no childhood and no parents. My father's moral concerns were nonexistent, and I heaped all of mine into Smiley. I think I made a bit of a new father out of him.

Interviewer: In *A Perfect Spy*, George is nowhere to be found. Is Smiley finished?
le Carré: He and I are on bad terms. He imposed a perception of life upon me which I'm tired of: I don't like writing through an old man's eyes, and the older I get the more scary it is to do so.

Interviewer: How do you feel about his absence?
le Carré: With Smiley gone I can go into other people's heads. While I was using him as the narrator I could only perceive people through his eyes. We [Cornwell and Smiley] had a wonderful time. And then Alec Guinness got him, made the two BBC series, and the consequence of that was that Smiley became confined by Guinness. He became the property of Guinness. Even Alec's voice, the dying fall [Cornwell perfectly mimicks the actor's voice] became a metaphor for Smiley. That's wonderful—but it isn't my guy because once you cast a fictional character you limit him to those features and that voice. Until then he's in everybody's imagination, and they find what they like. So I thought it was a good time to move on. When you have a love affair with a character, it is wonderful. It makes writing an enormous pleasure. But it shouldn't go on too long, like all the best love affairs.

Another reason for my impatience with George Smiley is that I am no longer able to resolve his excuses. There is something specious to me now about his moral posture. The notion of Smiley's was that he sacrificed his moral conscience so that decent, ignorant people could sleep at night. He goes through life saying, "I give up all my moral judgments; I take upon myself the lash of my own guilt." We Empire Babies were brought up thinking that we messed with things so that others could have clean hands. But I believe that someone who delivers up the responsibility for his moral conscience is actually someone who hasn't got one.

Interviewer: Would you go back to Joseph [the hero of *The Little Drummer Girl*] in a future novel?
le Carré: No, I'm finished with him. It's only with Smiley and his kind that I was able to go back to them.

Interviewer: In one review it was said that your cover is blown because *A Perfect Spy* is autobiographical in terms of relationship with your father.
le Carré: I was prepared to release parts of my life, which is a perfectly normal way of writing novels. I mean, the large Victorian novels were unashamedly autobiographical. Without Dickens's father we'd have no Macawber. I was prepared to go that far because I don't want to draw on those resources anymore. I was prepared to spend that amount of capital, if you will. What I've blown I suppose I've done with calculation, but I certainly haven't finished my armory.

The Secret Life of John le Carré

Stephen Schiff / 1989

Reprinted from *Vanity Fair*, 52 (June 1989), pp.146–50, 152, 154, 188–89.

He is at once a confirmed recluse and a social dazzler, a serious artist and a reliable manufacturer of best-sellers, a punctilious puritan and a twinkle-eyed swiller of numberless mid-day vodkas, none of which ever causes the slightest slur or stumble. He is, in short, dual, paradoxical, a double agent bristling with secrets and surprise. He even has two names: David Cornwell, the one he was born with and still goes by, and John le Carré, the one he invented to grace the covers of his novels, among them *The Spy Who Came in From the Cold*; *Tinker, Tailor, Soldier, Spy*; *Smiley's People*; *The Little Drummer Girl*; and *A Perfect Spy*. What does one do with such a bundle of contradictions?

Mostly, one walks.

We are sitting in the brightly rustic kitchen of his cliff-top home in Cornwall, England, and you can see the forward-march fever overtake him long before his immaculate politesse permits him to propose an outing. Delicately, he pushes his lunch plate aside; fretfully, he eyes your half-full wineglass—will he have to wait for his guest's final gulps? He can already sniff the turf and sea that await us, and now, his nostrils flaring, he sneaks a glance out the window, checking for thunderclouds. Yet, all the while, he is talking in that musical croon of his, talking, in this case, about the trip to the Soviet Union he made to research his buoyant new novel, *The Russia House*. The book, which is fleet, somewhat ragged, and often unexpectedly moving, imagines what a spy operation would be like in the age of *glasnost and perestroika*; it also examines what might happen if a good-hearted British agent found in Russia what Cornwell himself found during his travels there. By which I mean he fell in love with the place.

"I simply threw myself upon the Soviets," he purrs. "If there were parties, I went to the parties, and if people invited me, I went. The customary thing to do is to flirt with the refuseniks, the dissidents. But I kind of know about that stuff. So I was much more interested in staying within the system, because that is the reality." He reaches up and grasps his thick white forelock tightly in one hand, squeezing it as if there were some thought trapped inside that he might wring out. "I do think that the spirit of acceptance and sacrifice in the Soviet Union has produced a better man, better comradeship, and, strangely, a better, warmer life—albeit in prison—than we live outside."

What he's saying strikes me as odd, not just because his Soviet experience sounds so improbably romantic, but because the shoulder-to-shoulder comradeship he so relishes among the Russians is just the sort of indulgence he rarely allows himself. Even in pursuing his researches, he says, "the most important thing was to travel alone, because I knew I would have to *be* my protagonist, Barley. And I always do my researches alone, because you travel faster and better, and you can give yourself much more easily to people without the criticisms of a companion." Solitude is vital to him. Although he is happily married and has four sons (three by a previous marriage) and numerous devoted friends, seclusion has become not just an inclination but a kind of creed; he believes in it because it works. After all, the more unencumbered a spy is, the more nimbly he can infiltrate the world he is observing. And, as his friend the writer Michael Herr puts it, "David *is* a spy—he's the ultimate observer, the ultimate gatherer of data."

It is the richness of what he gathers and the supple language with which he conveys it that make David Cornwell, with Graham Greene, not only the finest spy novelist of this century, but one of the best novelists—of any kind—that we have. His books are far more than lickety-split yarns; they can be read as edgy comedies of manners, stories of seduction and betrayal that work like some gray subterranean reflection of the sunnier worlds of Trollope and Wharton and Austen. In Cornwell's hands the spy story becomes a gleaming laboratory in which our intricacies are dissected and our true natures laid bare. Reading him, we discover that we are all, like his secret agents, dissemblers selling our "covers" to the world; we are all, like his doom-haunted fieldmen and "Joes," ruined romantics longing to align ourselves with a cause, a passion, a virtue just out of reach. "A spy story is not just a spy story," he says with some heat. "It can be a love story, a story about engagement and escape, about the search for institutional integrity. And my great good fortune is that because it is also a spy story, I think that I have culled a much bigger readership than if I had taken those themes and written about the period pains of a suburban English housewife."

He eyes my wineglass, which, unfortunately, I haven't touched. Then a glance out the window, to where the gardener is dragging, by the armpits, an imperturbable stone Madonna toward its place amid his seaside shrubs. Cornwell grins at the spectacle. His face is crisp and pallid, handsome in a distinctively English way, and ruddy when he laughs. Although the hair has gone gray, the brows are still snarly red thickets, and he has a habit of pulling his head back when he talks, so that he seems to be delivering his wisdom from a regal height. His conversation comes in tumbles of metaphor, with oddly apt adjectives sprinkled in for crunch. And there is also about him something indefinably poignant, the aura of a man who has secreted something urgent and painful for a very long time.

I had been told that I would find him very like one of the characters in his novels. "He's extremely charming," says one publishing insider, "but he's also a real game player, a manipulator." And Michael Herr says, "Many people who knew Henry James felt that they were just so many specimens in James's laboratory, and as endearing as they found him, they could never shake that feeling that he saw them first and foremost to observe them. There's a little of that in David. I have seen him set up certain situations with a roomful of people and then sort of sit back and let them play themselves out. But it's never malicious. And I've never heard him put down anybody who didn't bloody well deserve it." If Cornwell is some sort of social slyboots, I see no sign of it. On the contrary, he seems so joyfully gregarious that his enforced isolation feels like a kind of asceticism; it's as though he thought it would make him stronger because it goes so sharply against his grain. But perhaps what I'm seeing is a changed man, a man who has only recently emerged from some self-imposed chrysalis. Certainly he's a wonderful, avid listener, quick to endorse and agree. And he likes to keep his companions entertained. "You go to a dinner party with David," says his friend the writer and poet Al Alvarez, "and he will put on a show for you. He always sings for his supper, in a very amusing way, telling stories tirelessly. I have been with him at parties where we've both been clearly bored out of our skulls, and David has never ever let up. He's terribly well mannered, but it's purely an act so the evening won't sink into some slough of despond."

Perhaps the brightest bauble in his bag of dinner-party tricks is his gift for mimicry. "He has an actor's instinct, and his imitations of people are extremely good," says his friend Sir Alec Guinness, who played Cornwell's most famous spy, George Smiley, in two celebrated television adaptations.

"He really *is* an actor, in my opinion." Sir Alec himself holds an esteemed place among the writer's specialties—Cornwell can capture not just the lugubrious Guinness monotone but also the odd air of disappointed majesty, of long-suffering noblesse oblige. And Cornwell has countless other arrows in his quiver, from Margaret Thatcher (and her husband, Denis) to Harold Macmillan to Simone Signoret ("My dear, you've simply *got* to do an autobiography. Because one makes *money* like you and I have never seen"). The mimic's ear, in fact, is part of what gives his fiction its almost Dickensian sweep and vividness. The books teem, and even the cameo characters speak in a way that enables us to map a universe behind the page: class structures, political histories, love lives. Cornwell doesn't just imitate his people, he lives inside their skins.

I have drained my glass by now, and with a brisk "Let's walk!" Cornwell bounds into the next room to fetch his outdoor togs. "Whippets!" he sings, and on cue his two bony dogs clatter in—actual whippets, by the way, and whippet-thin besides. Cornwell strides in behind them, grinning, and says, "They know only one trick, and I must show it to you." Then, in the high voice of nanny coaxing a child: "Whippets! I believe there's a *critic* nearby. I think we have a *critic*, whippets. *Critic!*" Whereupon, in unison, the skinny beasts begin to moan and pule and circle chaotically. They look genuinely distressed.

"I'll bet they'd do the same thing if you substituted the word 'cricket,'" I say.

"I'm *quite* sure they would," Cornwell replies soothingly. And then it's into a raincoat and mud boots, and craggy walking stick in hand, off he marches across the cliffs, his city-slicker guest flapping alongside.

"Down here the people know I'm a writer," he says as we puff along, "but they forgive me. They don't really regard what I do as work." Walking is Cornwell's passion—his exercise, his therapy, his workshop—and he owns several acres of windswept Cornish coastland on which to indulge it. Below us, the land plummets seaward, and you can see the famously treacherous Channel waves flogging the rocks; from here it's a four-hour hike along the cliffs to Land's End, England's southern- and westernmost outcropping. Cornwell and his wife, Jane, have slapped together three nineteenth-century farmer's cottages and a barn, painted them white, and decorated the insides with comfy sofas and paintings by such Cornish artists as Edwin Harris and Stanhope Forbes. There is another rambling home in London, near Hampstead Heath, but Cornwell ventures there only to "top up the batteries."

"I hate being there," he says, "and I don't use any of the cultural theme park that London offers, really. But there's enough of the urban rub up there to remind me: faces, voices—just to go down to the pub in Hampstead and listen, to get a whole fresh draft of language, and really to learn how the world is moving and how people are thinking. Down here you can live a very fey life if you want to. So I need the thorn in the britches that London provides."

But Cornwell has no use for London's literary life. "I won't get involved with the literary bureaucracy, because I know what bureaucracies are. I know how corporate opinion can replace individual responsibility, and I also know how unpleasant people can be in the aggregate, when often they're very pleasant individually. I now have almost no experience of English writers at all, and I don't like what I see of them in a group. I don't like the sight of them reviewing one another, and preening one another, and it's just our lowest common factor. And I think it's to do very often with the fact that what they really would like is a corporate entity where they can wander down the corridor and have a cup of coffee with somebody and chew the fat about the boss. They want to belong to a family, which is the way most other people live."

After every London stint, Cornwell hightails it back to the coastlands and works until "the spurt" runs dry. "I do my writing in the early morning and then walk in the afternoon, correct in the evening, and then I like to go to bed worrying about the book, to let the brain go on ticking." He is, in short, the resolute, almost anchoritic handmaiden of his art. And so is his wife, Jane, a soft-spoken, brown-haired, humorous woman whom he met when she was working for his British publisher, Hodder & Stoughton, and who now, after seventeen years of marriage, is his full-time amanuensis, typing for him (he writes with pen and ink and has never mastered the typewriter), ordering his business affairs, reading his copy, and, mostly, safeguarding his solitude. "David's life is a big operation," says Michael Herr. "Not many days go by without somebody wanting something from him. And Jane protects him—from hangers-on, from intrusion, from contractual oversights. She's not just a literary wife but a literary superstar's wife."

In fact, it was the sudden onslaught of superstardom that made Cornwell so insistent on retreat. It happened in 1963, when he was just thirty-one, and a callow, woefully inexperienced foreign-service officer. He had already written two slender novels, *Call for the Dead* (1961) and *A Murder of Quality* (1962), which had gone nowhere, and now he was working in Bonn and Berlin. There he unexpectedly found himself in the midst of one of the century's epochal events. "The first barbed-wire entanglements were going up—the wall, you know. And people were being brought out, and they were jumping out of windows, and there was shooting. For three or four nights I hardly slept, and I got into that extraordinary vortex, which you can get into at that age, of sleeplessness and crisis—you forget to eat and you forget to go to bed and you forget to shave. You are crazy-bright and capable of anything. And I just had this notion of a story about this beat-up agent runner trying to get his agents out of the East. I wrote it over about five weeks—I used to write on the ferry to Bonn—and then it was done, and I really knew it was very good of its sort, that it worked. And I sent my accountant a letter saying if ever I was worth £20,000 he should send me a cable and I would resign from the foreign service. He called me about six weeks later and said I could retire."

Forever. The book was called *The Spy Who Came in From the Cold*, and it revolutionized the genre; no less than Graham Greene called it "the best spy novel I have ever read." In its way, it marked a boundary between two eras: the era of God-is-on-our-side patriotism, of trust in government and in the morality of the West, and the era of paranoia, of conspiracy theory and suspicion of government, of moral drift. In *The Spy Who Came in From the Cold*, the gossamer bonds between men came to seem more substantial than the chains of nationalism and ideology, and what had once been a black-and-white world suddenly began to look morning-after gray. The reading public was ready. "People knew about defectors and spies," says Cornwell. "And what did we get as the literary reflection of that but Ian Fleming's magic carpet and a bunch of pretty girls and fast cars and a facile, chauvinist perception of nationhood. The whole James Bond ethic did nothing but paper over our doubts. And to come in with a novel which used the same furniture and really presented nothing *but* doubt, and in very romantic terms—that produced a market explosion."

The Spy Who Came in From the Cold topped the American best-seller list for fourteen consecutive months. But who was this John le Carré? David Cornwell scarcely knew himself, and he wasn't sure how much to tell. "I allowed myself to be lionized in America for about ten days, which was extremely intoxicating. Television shows, hostesses, offers of love, marriage, the world. And huge sums of money. Even if I wrote the telephone directory for three or four books, my future was assured. I felt terribly lonely, of course, because my marriage was really not ready to sustain this influx of money and fame. It was really quite unhappy by then. My first wife thought the fact that

I was writing was anti-family, which of course it was, it's anti-everything—the writing comes first. And then appalling self-doubt, self-hate, all the things that happen with instant success. A lot of women for a while. And a lot of careless involvements, wrong involvements, trying out one's identity in different contexts, and the writing being really the only thread. But the worst thing was that I went into my high-profile situation with two very big lies in my rucksack, two secrets that I felt I absolutely could not talk about."

Two secrets. The first, of course, was that he really was a spy, and had been one for years. "And so in those pathetic attempts at describing myself on the celeb circuit and chat shows and so on, I had to work up a fictional version of myself as the honest diplomat, translating all his problems into this mythical world of espionage. And I'm sure I did it very plausibly, but it was a load of absolute codswallop." Cornwell had, in fact, been a denizen of the covert world for a long time. He was first approached by the British secret service when he was still in his teens, and he served in intelligence during a stint with the British Army of Occupation in Austria. And at Oxford, where he read modern languages (graduating with First Class Honors in 1956), he maintained his intelligence contacts—he may even have spied on left-wing students there, as his alter ego Magnus Pym does in the largely autobiographical *A Perfect Spy*.

It was at Oxford that he met and married his first wife, Ann; she was "the girl next door, really," and the daughter of a Royal Air Force officer. And then, as if to further confirm his place in the Establishment, he took a job teaching languages at Eton, probably the most renowned public school in Britain. But all the while, he says, he was internally battling his inclinations toward respectability. "I wanted terribly to find myself an artistic life. I knew by the time I left Oxford that I had a very robust intellect, and I also knew that I was extremely impatient with most orthodox forms of earning a living, and that I had a restless creativity within me. At Eton, I filled my spare time with drawing." But an early attempt at writing and illustrating a children's book met with rejection, and Cornwell soon left Eton to rejoin the secret service—first MI5, the equivalent of our F.B.I., and then MI6, the equivalent of our C.I.A. It was a way of indulging his innate subversiveness and satisfying his yen for propriety at the same time.

Cornwell was astonished at the doubt and disarray he found within the secret world. Far from the glamour of gun-encrusted sports cars and gold-encrusted blondes, he found himself living the routine of a slug among slugs, a foot soldier in a furtive army of fumbling bureaucrats. Still, he was finally an honest-to-God spook, and though he never slinked over enemy borders or crammed cyanide pills beneath his dental caps, he did learn the "black arts"—silent killing, karate, and so forth—and he did recruit and run low-level agents. All the while, he was writing, mostly on the early-morning train to work, and as his first novels came out, he submitted them to his superiors to make sure that he was not exposing secrets or breaking Foreign Office regulations (he continued these submissions until 1986, when, with *A Perfect Spy*, he decided "I was out of quarantine"). Of course, no intelligence functionary could be permitted to write about the secret service under his own name, and Cornwell decided to call himself John le Carré. "I made up some story about having seen it from the top of a bus on a shoe shop. It may be true, but I don't think so. I just got sick of saying, 'I don't know where it came from.' Tactically speaking, I thought that a name by a Brit that had John in it and three parts looked rather good; it had a certain force. So it's all a little tiny deception operation."

Cornwell insists that he hasn't maintained contacts within the active intelligence community, that he hasn't kept up with the technology, that he's no expert on contemporary espionage. All of which makes his accomplishment the more remarkable. For the "wilderness of mirrors" he has extrapolated from his years on the inside is as powerfully imagined a creation as any in our literature, a universe with its own detailed physics and moral laws, even its own infectious jargon: the "moles," "honey traps," "pavement artists," and so forth—evocative terms, some of which were actually in use in the covert world and some of which Cornwell invented, only to discover, much later, that real-life spies had adopted them after reading his books. Most important of all, Cornwell learned how to reason like a spook, learned the "inside-out thinking" that gives his plots their diverting complexity: how do you fool people who know you are trying to fool them, and know that you know that they know, and so forth? "It's the mentality that a good mind naturally acquires in the intelligence service," says Cornwell. "After a few years, that's the way you start to think. And the rest is a reworking. After I left, I kind of re-recruited all those notions and memories and turned them into a private bestiary."

But how accurate are Cornwell's depictions of modern espionage? The writer himself doesn't know. "And besides, I don't need authenticity," he says. "I need credibility—seeming authenticity." Phillip Knightley, who was the last western journalist to interview Kim Philby before the spy's death in Moscow last year, says that "Philby read every le Carré book and enjoyed them all up to *The Honorable Schoolboy* in 1977. After that, they suddenly became more complicated than any intelligence operation in which Philby had ever been involved." Knightley, however, finds Cornwell's fictional intrigues perfectly believable, and so does Cornwell's friend the writer William Shawcross. "David was having supper at my house in the country," he says, "and Denis Healey [the former defense secretary] came to supper, too. And Healey said to David, 'The things you write—one might think you worked for the K.G.B.!' Which was an outrageous thing to say, but the purport was that David was exposing a lot of things that were extremely true about the way in which the British secret service works."

What is unquestionably true in the books is their depiction of the way men behave together (espionage, despite the advances of feminism, is still a man's world). Men fall in love with each other in these novels, instantly, ferociously; they become the victims of thralldoms and crushes that have nothing to do with eroticism and everything to do with the sort of madness to which boys separated from girls are prone. "You get these very close relationships among men," Cornwell explains, "which result from the excitement of shared operations, from a collective mythos. And the attractions of a big operation are often: Hooray, I can call home and say [suddenly shifting into the voice of a distracted yuppie], 'Um, sorry, dear. Been in with the Big Man, rather a thing come up. Shan't be back for three weeks.' It's great—'*You* look after the fucking children!' And it is absolutely ludicrous to imagine, for example, that a couple hundred men in a nuclear submarine that is going to be underwater for six months cannot go collectively mad. The idea that because one guy's got the key and the other guy's got the key and the third guy's got the key, that all three of them could never go mad together and push the nuclear button is ridiculous. It's exactly what they *will* do. Insanity is contagious. That's how you get the Bay of Pigs. That's how you get the abortive attempt to liberate the Iranian hostages. You get one of these male saint figures up front and you begin to get the unreal, self-driving force of men feeding off each other. That's always been a very strong part of what I've written about."

He stops and grabs his forelock again—a gesture, I recall, in which many of his characters indulge. We are sitting now in his living room, drinking champagne in the early afternoon; icy vodka will follow. We have been talking

about passionate attachments between men, and now it is time to talk about
Cornwell's other big secret, the one he's wrestled with all his life. It is time to
talk about his father.

Bits of Ronald Cornwell had shown up in *The Honourable Schoolboy* and
The Little Drummer Girl, and even earlier and more explicitly in *The Naive
and Sentimental Lover* (1971), le Carré's biggest flop, and the only one of his
novels that isn't about spies. *The Naive and Sentimental Lover* is a veiled but
revealing account of Cornwell's tempestuous friendship with the late writer
James Kennaway and of his involvement with Kennaway's beautiful wife,
Susan. (Kennaway, the author of the celebrated novel *Tunes of Glory*, had
explored the same stormy romantic triangle in his 1967 novel, *Some Gorgeous
Accident*.) In *The Naive and Sentimental Lover*, Cornwell's fictional stand-in is
a wealthy bourgeois pram manufacturer whose father is a bit of a nut, a per-
petually penniless ne'er-do-well and a con man who could charm rain from
the desert sky. When Ronald Cornwell heard about the book, he threatened
to sue his son (a threat he would make again later, after David gave a TV
interview that, in his father's opinion, failed to grant old Ronnie enough
credit for his son's success). But in fact Cornwell's depictions of his father
were relatively mild. For the real Ronald Cornwell was not merely a likable
scamp. He was an epic con man, a supernally charming liar and thief whose
escapades left a wake of chaos and pain that still ripples through the younger
Cornwell's life—even though Ronnie died nearly fourteen years ago.

When David Cornwell was born, in October 1931, Ronnie and his wife,
Olive, were living in the Dorset coastal town of Poole, and for a few years
Ronnie managed to surround his young son with a mirage of prosperity. But
when David was six, his father was imprisoned for fraud (and not for the last
time); his mother left home soon afterward, never contacting her son again
until he was in his twenties. Ronnie continued, however sporadically, to care
for David and his older brother. But despite all the fancy cars and fancy
houses and fancy hangers-on, despite all the racehorses and rambunctious
parties and flirtations with countesses and queens, the boys soon discovered—often through surreptitious perusal of the old man's private papers—
that their father was living an enormous lie. He once sent his teenage sons to
Paris to pick up his golf clubs at the posh George V hotel; when they got
there they found that the golf clubs had been left "as surety for his bill." On
another occasion, when Ronnie couldn't pay up at a luxurious hotel in St.
Moritz, he convinced the management that he had decided to buy the place,

that all the parties and lavish dinners he'd enjoyed there had been staged to test the hotel's services; in the end, his bills were forgotten. Ronnie managed to maintain fleets of cars, myriad phony companies (each with its own letterhead), spacious offices in pricey Jermyn Street—and police records in such far-flung capitals as Singapore and Jakarta. And as the young David grew accustomed to inventing fibs about his father's whereabouts—and excuses to explain his father's inability to pay for his schooling (except, occasionally, in black-market fruit)—he found himself becoming a virtuoso in the arts of subterfuge and sham. He became a kind of princeling in the kingdom of the clandestine, a born defector and double agent—a perfect spy.

It was the horror of being his father's son that led Cornwell to despise one of his most resplendent gifts—his charm. "I've put my charm in places that I'm ashamed of," he says now, "and I have at times attracted loyalty on a scale that appalled me, without wishing to do so. I have revelations of myself when I was young and ruthless as somebody who did make indiscriminate use of his seductive powers, not towards women but in work. Somebody who allowed his humanity to be misused."

We have hit upon a subject that makes him uncomfortable, and he squirms for a moment in his chair. It's as though he viewed his charm as a kind of destructive emanation, a beam radiating from him unbidden, which he must take great pains to control. "It's a matter of finding the bits of oneself which match the bits of the other person you're talking to. It's clear to me that I have that, and it's sincere—I think so. The difficulty always is to get people out of my life, to wrestle myself free enough to write. You know, everybody spoke of my father's charm, the art of making people do impossible things. And charm in the secret world is placed very high on the list of desirable qualities. It's called, in recruitment terms, 'entertainment value.' And at its baldest, it means that your wretched little agent, stuck somewhere, is actually going to look forward to seeing you. He or she is run-down, exhausted, lying to her employers, and she wants to be turned into a goddess for the evening, and she wants to be listened to—she wants a confessor. In other words, the very attributes which in my father I tended to perceive as larcenous were the ones which my employers found attractive in me. So I've got it in for charm. Charm's on my hit list."

Ronnie's legendary charm pursued David like a wraith. When the younger Cornwell became the famous John le Carré, his father was suddenly everywhere, calling himself Ron le Carré, promising the head of a Berlin film studio the rights to the latest of his son's books, even pretending to be the famous author himself, and not just for business purposes but also to enhance his fly-by-night amours. And yet, somehow, David was able to keep the secret of his father's enormities to himself. He tried to write about Ronnie from time to time, and when he failed he filled his novels with worthier substitute fathers—most spectacularly George Smiley, the chubby and mild-mannered cuckold who also happens to be the cleverest and most powerful spy in Britain. In fact, there was a time when Cornwell believed he would never again attempt a book that didn't feature Smiley. But Alec Guinness's portrayals in TV's *Tinker, Tailor, Soldier, Spy* and *Smiley's People* changed all that. "I mean, Guinness had taken over the part," says Cornwell, smiling ruefully, "and his voice was in my ear, and it wasn't Smiley's voice. I was writing Guinness cadences, and giving him Guinness mannerisms, and Alec had done it so wonderfully—he's such an old thief. It wasn't my Smiley, it was his Smiley." Cornwell finally left Smiley out of the picture altogether in *The Little Drummer Girl*, and that cleared the way at last for the big book about his father and himself, the book that is and may always be Cornwell's masterpiece—the book so aptly called *A Perfect Spy*.

At the end of 1986, the year of its publication, Philip Roth called *A Perfect Spy* "the best English novel since the war," and though that judgment may strike one as immoderate, it suggests the book's breadth and power. In painting a portrait of his own upbringing and recruitment into the covert world, Cornwell also created, in Rick Pym, a father figure as vigorous, likable, and despicable as any in recent memory. *A Perfect Spy* moves at a more measured pace than we are used to from le Carré, but it slices deeper. A spy story and even a thriller, it's also one of the most penetrating depictions in all literature of the links between love and betrayal—Cornwell's constant theme—and it's set against an enormous Hogarthian canvas of scoundrels, innocents, nymphomaniacs, prigs, aristocrats, servants, and spooks, many of whom kick their way to the forefront of the reader's consciousness, make their indelible impression, and then neatly disappear. Reading *A Perfect Spy*, one can't help but feel the liberating surge Cornwell must have experienced as he finally emptied his rucksack of secrets. The exultation and horror of confession mingle on every page.

And then what? What happens after you write the masterpiece that has been burning inside you since you first set pen to paper? "Getting that monkey off my back was a tremendous catharsis for me," Cornwell replies, "and

I cried and cried when it was over. And though I've never been to a shrink, I think that writing *A Perfect Spy* is probably what a very wise shrink would have advised me to do anyway. But then I did have all these feelings that maybe I had finished my writing career. I felt I had touched the limits of my ability in *A Perfect Spy*, and that I was in danger of contemplating my navel for too long, getting stage fright, and perhaps doing a Heller[1] or a David Lean—just going off the map for ten or twelve years. And so it seemed to me very important to put another card down fast, to keep up the ease of narrative in a way, to keep up the energy, the thrust. And then I thought, Well, I'll get off my ass and I'll find Russia. So I wrote *The Russia House*—and really enjoyed writing it."

It shows. *The Russia House* is not the sort of lapidary work *A Perfect Spy* and *The Little Drummer Girl* were, but it has a jubilant zing neither of those novels possesses. The story follows a familiar le Carré pattern: an ordinary man is seduced into spying, his masters set an operation in motion, and then, slowly but surely, the very traits that they have misperceived or overlooked in their new recruit come bubbling to the surface, overwhelming the operation and, eventually, the spy himself. In a book like le Carré's *The Looking-Glass War*, that pattern of events can feel crushing, but in *The Russia House* it has almost the opposite effect. When le Carré's hero, Barley, goes haywire, it's not because he is succumbing to the bleak inevitability that le Carré's Fates usually impose; instead, he is loosing the fetters of nation and destiny, releasing himself into an exuberant romanticism that is stranger and more thrilling than anything else he has known. (*The Russia House* may make an even better movie than novel; Tom Stoppard is working on the screenplay, and the director Fred Schepisi plans to begin shooting in the Soviet Union in September.)[2]

"I think I know it's an untidy book," Cornwell admits, "but I'm very pleased with the heart of it. And I'm very pleased to be publishing it, because the book in its way was also a bridge I had to cross to go to something else— the *Urbuch*, as the Germans say: the book of books." Cornwell stops for a moment, and slowly, contemplatively, pours himself another vodka—the stuff is so cold it has thickened into a kind of alcoholic broth. A wistfulness has settled over him now, and I'm seeing a side that perhaps he would never have allowed himself to show an outsider in the old days—the days of the

---

1. Joseph Heller's *Catch-22* appeared in 1961 and his *Something Happened* in 1974; but he published two plays in the interim.
2. The movie appeared in 1990.

secrets. "I do think the two lies were a tremendous weight upon me," he says, "and I wrote almost physically like that, cramped and with a tremendous concern for accuracy, for laying out perfect steps of narrative and so on. *A Perfect Spy* really cracked me wide open. I came dangerously close to a portrait of my own secret life, and it left me feeling artistically a great deal better. I was able to get more of the genie out of the box, and that gave me more voices as a narrator, and opened me up much more to the possibilities of the novel." He looks at me studiously, his eyes very wide and still; all the tension has drained from his face. "I have at this moment a tremendous joy," he says. "I feel that I have found my voice, like a singer. I know I'm hitting the right notes, the notes I want."

Is he ready, then, for the *Urbuch*? "Yes, I think that's what I would like to do now. I think my next book is going to take me four or five years, and I'd like to start it as soon as possible.[3] I'd like to have nothing else to do at all, and I'd like to start the research, start living it a bit."

His voice throbs. "I've defected from the two secrets, you see, and I think the defector in me is satisfied." And then he says something very strange, strange for one of the world's most successful writers, stranger still for a man who has revolutionized a genre—but not so strange, perhaps, for a novelist as devoted to the tender cultivation of his talent as David Cornwell. "I think I know how to write now, at last," he says, very softly. "I do think my apprenticeship is finally over."

3. *The Secret Pilgrim*—a collection of stories—was published in 1990; *The Night Manager* was published in 1993.

The Thawing of the Old Spymaster

Alvin P. Sanoff / 1989

Reprinted from *U.S. News & World Report*, 106 (19 June 1989), pp. 59–61.
Copyright © 1989, *U.S. News & World Report*, L.P. Reprinted by permission.

le Carré: We are living through absolutely extraordinary times; we're back in 1918 again. The current Soviet experiment is over, and we've achieved the ideological discrediting of Bolshevism. But we must realize that, mentally, we too are casualties of the cold war. We have gotten into a mode of thinking that suggests there is no solution, that all we can do is live with the slogans we have created.

I don't think we ever supposed that in our lifetime we would be talking about the visible crumbling of power in the Soviet Union, the fragmentation of the empire, the possibility of a Soviet commonwealth. Now, great themes are being forced upon us. The question is: Can we undergo our *perestroika* and produce the leaders to meet the situation, or will we go on dancing to the music of the past long after that music has ceased?

Interviewer: Might some people contend that the cynical le Carré has simply gone soft?

le Carré: Perhaps it takes somebody who has chronicled the cynicism for so long to point to new possibilities. The realist in me is perfectly aware that this is not the time to unbuckle our guns. We can hang on to the big stick, but we must reach out with new ideas as well. Either we help the Soviets out of the ice and turn them into the kind of business and political partner that we need, or we miss the opportunity and precipitate a return, more or less, to the cold war. For many people, the maintenance of the status quo would be a great convenience.

It's very dangerous to approach the peace with the same people who've been fighting the cold war. In fact, the cold war happened because we moved from the hot war to the cold war with the same team on both sides. The manners of open hostility became the manners of covert hostility.

It requires a great statesman on our side; we have to find the other half of Gorbachev.[1]

Interviewer: How will the changes in the Soviet Union affect your novels?
le Carré: If the Soviet Union and the client states on its western borders are in such ferment, then we need all the intelligence we can get about every bird that's singing in every tree. So spying will continue apace, though its flavor and purposes may be more benign. The spy story will find a new identity according to the new winds that blow. After all, the spy story existed in Somerset Maugham and Joseph Conrad long before the cold war. To imagine that writers have to freeze a political situation in order to function is simply to discredit the trade.

The early period of the cold war had James Bond as its literary champion, and that was an absolute travesty of reality; it was an absurdity and a vulgarity. What it created was a great appetite for a countermarket that I and others supplied. So, although the changes may break Tom Clancy's begging bowl for a bit, I don't write that kind of book. I have written about people caught in an endless ideological gridlock. Now, I just feel a great sense of relief. The future is mine to play with, as a whole new realm of imaginative speculation opens up.

Interviewer: How do you manage to keep up with what goes on in the world of intelligence?
le Carré: I just imagine it. If it were otherwise, I wouldn't lie to you. I have no sources; I know nothing. But it's like this: If a veteran journalist gave up his work tomorrow, even twenty years from now he could pick up a magazine or newspaper and sense instantly the way that paper is structured and why stories are handled in a certain way. So, when I see something occur in the world of intelligence, I get a kind of imaginative readout of what probably happened—and, quite likely, it's right.

It has always been my concern not to be authentic but to be credible, to use the deep background I have from the years I spent in intelligence work to present premises that were useful to my stories and that I knew were rooted in experience. It's terribly easy to imagine an operational context when you've done a few operations; it's as if you were asking a sailor how he kept up with the sea. Of course, what I didn't know I just made up.

---

1. Mikhail Gorbachev (1931–), who became General Secretary of the Soviet Communist Party in 1985, launched a period of "glasnost" (openness) and "perestroika" (political transformation) in the U.S.S.R.

Interviewer: Do people who are still in intelligence work ever come to you and say, "Gee, how did you know that?"

le Carré: I can't think of any instance where that's happened except in *The Little Drummer Girl.* Although I met only a couple of former chiefs of the Mossad, it was easy for me to imagine the importance of intelligence to the Israelis and to imagine, much in the British manner, how you recruit, where you get your best people from and how the Old Boy network works. Israelis later told me that I had got it right, insofar as one ever gets it right.

But one must remember with these outfits that nobody really has a bird's-eye view: Everybody's experience is tangential. Everybody working in intelligence imagines more or less that there's a real intelligence service somewhere else, so that they are, in a sense, as gullible as the average reader. As long as I remain true to the grammar they know, they'll accept most theses as being likely.

Interviewer: Your novels have been less than kind to Americans.

le Carré: The people I've really been nastiest to are the Brits. If my Americans at times seem crude, it's because sometimes American political actions have also seemed crude. That has occurred because America is where the power is. A nation isn't always popular when it exercises power and makes grave decisions. Americans, too, are enormously concerned about their own political manners and are repeatedly embarrassed by what they see as acts of grossness by their leaders.

Although in the Brit tradition, spying is waiting, watching, listening and painfully accurate reporting, quite often in the United States the impulse to action is almost greater than the impulse to wait and think. The Bay of Pigs and "Irangate" mainly were operations that failed for want of real analysis. It's in the American character to say that if you know something, you had better do something about it. That is not the British way. We spend years measuring the strength and length and width of the ropes that may hang us, but we don't hire great quantities of clandestine rope cutters to go and chop them up.

Interviewer: Many of the Americans in your new book are not comfortable with the recent changes in the Soviet Union.

le Carré: The United States has established a military-industrial complex in which, I believe, about forty percent of the engineers are engaged in defense-related work. So there are those who have a vested interest in the continuation of the status quo. In the West, all the checks and balances of democratic procedure militate against swift change, and the vulnerability of public life to vested interests turns us into a slower-moving dinosaur at the moment than the Soviet Union, where the government can impose revolution from above. Economically speaking, the Soviets have very little to lose and much to save.

Interviewer: Did the idea for your new book, *The Russia House*, come as a result of your trip to the Soviet Union in 1987?
le Carré: For more than a quarter of a century, I've been referring to the Soviet Union from outside. So, when I had the chance, I went out of curiosity—to be there at an extraordinary time in history and see for myself. On my first visit, I had a very misty idea of my leading character and leading woman. But I just let myself be blown around by whatever winds caught me. And then between a visit in May and a second visit in September, I put together the rudiments of my story. I knew that I would freeze it historically in 1987. If Gorbachev caught a bad bullet or another Brezhnev returned, I would still have my little fable set in that time and wouldn't be indecently running after tomorrow's news.

What I did not expect, though I should have imagined it, was that the Soviet people's cultural perceptions of Europe are virtually stuck in the nineteenth century because so little of modern literature has reached them. Their education has been safely oriented around the classics. People talk to you endlessly about Thomas Hardy, William Thackeray and Jane Austen because such works were politically undangerous in childhood. I found the notion of a time warp very moving.

I also realized that I was of the menopausal generation of men who are making all this happen in the Soviet Union—the guys in their late fifties who exercise power, who have been through Stalin, even if they remember it as occurring in their late childhood and early twenties. Then they experienced the heady promise of Khrushchev, the belief that they might be coming out of the ice. Then—bang!—Brezhnev and into the freeze again. And now a real spring, with all the complexities and massive problems that they face.

Interviewer: You suggest in the book that we overestimate the Soviet military capability.
le Carré: The larger and more risky assumption that I made after returning from the Soviet Union was that a country so congenitally inefficient, extraordinarily incompetent and frequently lazy could not nurse at its center a flawless, superefficient military capability. There is now ample evidence to bear out that conjecture.

If an equally underdeveloped Third World country took it upon itself to produce a Rolls-Royce, the incompetence factor would come through again and again. That's what happens in the Soviet system. I'm no defense expert; it's just a human perception that you cannot actually circumscribe incompetence. You can't make a corral in the middle of such a chaotic state and say, "Inside here, everything will work perfectly." Of course, if you're in the defense business, you've got to assume the worst all the time; that's the game. But it's not the reality.

Interviewer: Have you begun another book?

le Carré: I'm superstitious about even indicating that unwritten books are in the pipeline, let alone talking about what's in those books. But I think that I have discovered a new voice—or rediscovered an old one. I wrote *The Russia House* in a much friskier, leaner style—more in the manner of *The Spy Who Came in From the Cold* but with all the experience that I've picked up in the years between.

I had a great battle with my preceding novel, *A Perfect Spy*. I had wanted to write it for years, and it finally seemed to come right—it was a great release. I came out of my own ice, so to speak, with a feeling that I had completed the cycle of all those novels. It was a pre-*perestroika* book, if you will. I was very much aware that the whole epoch that I had been trying to chronicle was in some way running out and that even the suicide at the end was somehow symbolic of the end of that kind of writing and that kind of hopelessness. So, understandably, I rushed to embrace the possibility of a new era both in my own mood and in the mood of the world around me.

Interviewer: Where is your master spy George Smiley now?

le Carré: He's in retirement, and we barely speak. Maybe we will get together later—I'll do some short stories or a Smiley book—but, at the moment, I'm very happy without him. I find him inhibiting because of his age and his pessimism and also the limitations of his sexuality. How many times can you cuckold your main character without its becoming a cliché of the business?

I do think that he would be cautiously cheerful and very surprised about what is happening in the Soviet Union. And while he would feel that we have to be careful in our dealings, he would also say, "Let's, for heaven's sake, go for it because we've tried the other and it didn't work."

What Would I Be Like If I Were He?

Der Spiegel / 1989

Reprinted from *Der Spiegel*, no. 32 (7 August 1989), pp. 143–48. Copyright © *Der Spiegel*. Reprinted by permission. Translated by Ursula and Horst Kruse.

Interviewer: John le Carré, as your new thriller, *The Russia House*, has it, intelligence services are no panacea, but rather an illness. Is this a moment of truth for the former spy, John le Carré?

le Carré: The statement is made by a character in my book, and what he means is this: the constant dealings with secret material can also stimulate the use of secret material. For instance, when I am in charge of an intelligence service department with a killer at its disposal, you can be sure that in the back of my mind I am looking for a suitable victim. The means become the end.

Interviewer: To be an intelligence service agent, does that give you a sense of superiority?

le Carré: At the time when I was one, it did. It is the feeling of being the only person with a pistol in his pocket—although I did not actually carry one. It is the feeling of belonging to an elite that does questionable things so that the average person can sleep in peace. An heroic self-image.

Interviewer: And the questionable things are sanctified . . .

le Carré: . . . with medals, yes. You are doing the questionable things also because the criminal side of your nature is called upon. It is an enormous pleasure to organize a burglary with the support of your government. A double pleasure.

Interviewer: Is it true that you were hired by the secret intelligence service even as a teenager?

le Carré: I cannot talk about what I did in this secret world and when I did it. I also believe that one should not talk about it.

Interviewer: Would you agree—once a spy, always a spy?
le Carré: It is true that for nearly thirty years I haven't had anything to do with the world of intelligence service; I avoid its company. But it is also true that its way of thinking, its way of reacting has stayed with me. Once a spy, always a spy—I believe that is perfectly true. And I do not know if I am a writer who turned spy or a spy who eventually turned writer.

Interviewer: Literature thus is a continuation of espionage by other means?
le Carré: Exactly. I believe that most writers, regardless of whether they are spies or not, feel themselves to be in a state of alienation. They are part of society, but separate from it; they deceive the people whom they depend on. They have to have the trust of their environment, but at the same time to keep at a distance from it and report on it.

There was an English writer who said, "Never leave me alone in your study, for I am sure to read your correspondence." What Graham Greene refers to as the "ice splinter" in the heart of a writer one could also call "the spy in him."

Interviewer: The superb scenes of interrogation in your books, those jungle wars in depth-psychology, do we owe them as well to your past with the secret intelligence service?
le Carré: I conducted many interrogations, certainly, and I love this method because of its suspense and its enigmatic quality. It is the ultimate method of character investigation and a mirror-game: the only pieces of information that I have about the other person are within myself. In other words: what would I be like if I were he?

Interviewer: Doppelgänger, thou pale companion: Is that it?
le Carré: When, as a writer, I spied on myself, I often invented characters that represented the other half of me. But the business of espionage also produces protagonists: the Cold War was a contest of things imagined, of phantasms; we were forever inventing, for instance during the missiles race, monstrous numbers and motives with the enemy, and then responding to these.

Interviewer: When le Carré the writer spied on himself, did he similarly uncover secrets?
le Carré: The interplay between experience and creativity is a mystery that we ourselves cannot penetrate. But the greatest magic of writing lies in the fact

that one actually does not know oneself as long as things have not been put on paper. That is what renews the urge to write. It is a journey of discovery into the self.

Interviewer: Have you come to know yourself well by now?
le Carré: I find myself, like most people, endlessly surprising and fascinating.

Interviewer: After your first interlude with the secret intelligence service and after a career in the university, you returned to the haven of British intelligence. Why?
le Carré: I think I was attracted by the idea of penetrating to a secret center, to what actually makes up the world in its essence. In my quest for a moral institution I believed that somewhere in the heart of the brotherhood of intelligence the key was to be found to our identity, to our collective desires and to our destiny. I believed that there I would find the blue flower of Romanticism.

I was attracted by the idea of putting the component parts of my nature into the hands of one single authority, of finding a place where my disorganized talents would be put in order. I grew up in the decline of the tradition of the Empire, and I believe I considered our secret intelligence service to be the last church of this Empire theology.

Interviewer: You suspect that intelligence could be a kind of substitute religion?
le Carré: I believe that is true. As a spy in the field, an operative spy, you have to believe in the virtue of a higher power. You have to believe in the benevolence of the people that control you. You have to have the moral strength to be completely self-sufficient, like a monk. You cannot indulge your weaknesses or make compromises concerning your calling.

Interviewer: But the spies in your books, your legendary Smiley, for instance, are also great doubters, aren't they?
le Carré: Yes, but Smiley wrestles with his doubts as a religious believer. To use a religious metaphor: he believes in Rome, knowing quite well, however, that Rome is corrupt. And the purity of his faith is frequently greater among those on assignment than among those at headquarters—which is quite normal for churches.

Interviewer: Have such doubts also befallen the spy le Carré?

le Carré: Yes, there were times in which personal morals were at odds with those of the patriot. And there were times in which it seemed impossible to do good work because the employers' incompetence became all too obvious. Nevertheless, you have to be loyal; the alternative is treason.

Interviewer: Treason—a central topic with John le Carré. Have you ever been a traitor yourself?

le Carré: The truth is that at that time, as a member of the secret intelligence service, I did things in good faith that now I am ashamed of. And that means that I am now in a way betraying the principles to which I had formerly subscribed. Treason is a product of development.

Interviewer: Does that mean that without treason one cannot survive?

le Carré: I think it was Goethe who called life a series of engagements and escapes; one could also call it a sequence of engagement and treason. We all know the feeling, don't we, when we look back on the women we once loved: how could I have been the man to be in love with this person? Who was it that I was then? A total mystery. Unswerving loyalty is a sterile thing.

Interviewer: Barley, too, the protagonist of your new novel, clearly vacillates between loyalty and treason . . .

le Carré: . . . true, and whom should he be loyal to? In his life Barley reaches the point at which he discovers the only loyalty there is—loyalty towards the intensity of one's own feelings.

Interviewer: Once again something religious, in a way, isn't it?

le Carré: Yes, it is. I think one difference between Graham Greene and myself, apart from the fact that he is the much better writer . . .

Interviewer: Objection, Your Honor . . .

le Carré: . . . is that Greene could always turn to God with his solutions. I have always described a wilderness that has been deserted by God—if he was ever actually there. Resolutions take place within persons and within the drama itself; no deus ex machina descends to take care of the business.

Interviewer: Does a spy have to be a patriot, at least?

le Carré: No. Intelligence is a microcosm of the world at large; it contains all kinds of motives. You can spy out of love, out of hatred, out of patriotism, out of disappointment, for fun, because life is tedious, or because you want to feel superior to other people.

Interviewer: You are thinking of James Bond, probably.
le Carré: Yes, but I have never actually seen Bond as a spy. Rather, I consider him to be a child of the western economic miracle, with a license for extreme misbehavior in the interest of capital.

Interviewer: Intelligence services being a microcosm, don't they also represent the collective unconscious of a people?
le Carré: That is exactly the way I use them in my books, as a theater of the national character. And it is fair to say that in the Soviet Union, in Israel, and in my own country conspiratorial activity is intricately intertwined with upper-class social behavior. Not so in the United States: whereas we inherited a secret-service society, the Americans had to invent one. So what you have in the USA is a kind of artificially constructed patriotism, which is often invested in the CIA.

Interviewer: The Germans, according to what you say in your books occasionally, are incomplete. What do you mean by that?
le Carré: What I mean is that there is a vivid longing in them, an unfulfilled sense of community, and that history has left them standing alone with that feeling.

Interviewer: Fifty years ago they did have a feeling of fulfillment.
le Carré: They did have the fulfillment, but it was no success.

Interviewer: There is a German lady whom you feel quite close to . . .
le Carré: . . . who stimulated and encouraged me immensely in my young years: indeed, the German muse. It was through her that I became a turncoat, a traitor for the first time. For at sixteen I ran away from my English school. I persuaded my father to send me to Bern, where I attended the university and threw myself completely into the arms of German culture.

Interviewer: Even though that was immediately after Hitler.
le Carré: That was all the more exciting, naturally, since it had the fascination of the forbidden. At that time I absolutely refused to speak English and to

identify myself as an Englishman. A very childish revenge upon my country. Later at Oxford I was a very serious student of German literature for a period of four years; after that I taught modern languages at Eton for two years.

At that time I had completely immersed myself in classic German literature, and I believe it continued to be the strongest formal influence: I did not love Keats and Shelley, but Büchner and Lenz, their neurotic despair. I was also enchanted, in a romantic fashion, by the German Middle Ages; I still consider the *Nibelungenlied* to be one of the greatest literary creations.

No German writer takes up his pen without asking the fundamental question of being. I, too, have something of this "quest for the absolute" in me; for a time I even wrote poems in German, which—the Lord be praised— I have lost.

Interviewer: They were certainly in the manner of Rilke, weren't they?
le Carré: Naturally I loved Rilke very much. As a young man I visited his grave, in this tiny cemetery beside a factory in a small town not far from Bern.

Interviewer: Thomas Mann, however, you still found among the living.
le Carré: In 1949 in Bern; he was giving the official address on the bicentennial of Goethe's birth. I was so full of enthusiastic feelings that I went to his backstage room and knocked at the door. Thomas Mann, who looked like the actor Clifton Webb, opened the door and said, "What do you want?" I said, "I would like to shake your hand." He said, "Here it is."

Interviewer: Your immersion in German literature explains why your spy Smiley adores German Baroque literature, and why Grimmelshausen's *Simplicissimus* even plays a central role in your *A Perfect Spy*, namely as a code book. Isn't Simplicissimus anyway a kind of model figure for you?
le Carré: That is true, a childlike, innocent person who ends up in absolute chaos and experiences suffering. During the war in Cambodia, when I did research in Phnom Penh for my book *The Honourable Schoolboy*, I myself ended up in a Simplicissimus-like situation, and I experienced for the first time the "majesty of suffering." I kneeled beside a dying soldier, and I saw children go to war. It was a turning-point in my life.

Interviewer: Wasn't *A Perfect Spy*, your fictive autobiography, a similar turning-point, an unmasking?

le Carré: To invoke Goethe once more: it is my *ur*-book, the book of books, for it destroyed the two great windmills in my life. One was my father, a confidence man, a monster, of whom I was thus able to rid myself. And the other was the fact that I used an institution, the intelligence service, as a substitute father, as womb to experience my belated childhood. After the book I was a new person, much happier.

Interviewer: Also drained by writing, perhaps?

le Carré: A life had ended, and a new one was beginning, a wonderful future, and, curiously, all of this coincided with a change in the world, glasnost and perestroika, about which I have written in *The Russia House*.

Interviewer: Le Carré, shoulder to shoulder with the Hegelian *Weltgeist*?

le Carré: A large term, but yes, that's the way I feel about it.

Interviewer: Just a few years ago you pleaded for "fighting Communism with resolution"; the Moscow *Literaturnaja Gaseta* denounced you as a Cold War provocateur. Has glasnost softened you?

le Carré: My aversion to Soviet Communism was humanist, for it did terrible things to people in the name of an ideology. It was for this reason that I considered it to be an abominable doctrine. Glasnost has convinced me that this is not the actual problem any longer.

Interviewer: Your *Russia House* is set in large part in Moscow and Leningrad, and as usual you did on-site research. How did you find that?

le Carré: When I traveled to the Soviet Union two years ago, I found myself in a huge debating club, in an atmosphere of creative enthusiasm; the Russians love ideas, and with them, ideas often replaced action. Everybody wanted to talk with the visitor from the West.

I immediately discovered a natural affinity with people of my own age, people who had gone along with compromises, who had suffered disappointments, and who now suddenly had revolution foisted on them. I, too, had struck compromises; I, too, had been a Cold War proponent. And so we understood each other like veterans.

I was totally overwhelmed by the familiarity with the classics among the Soviet intellectuals, and there was an anachronism that was truly exciting: their German was of archaic dignity, their English as from a novel by Jane Austen. Their longing is for the old Europe, but their destiny unfortunately will be the American model.

Interviewer: Graham Greene, whom you like to quote, also a former intelligence service person, used to avail himself of his visits to Moscow to meet a former colleague, double agent Kim Philby. Philby, who has since died, is said to have been eager to welcome you as well.
le Carré: I refused to meet him, for I always held him to be a perfectly disgusting person. To this day no one realizes what havoc he created by delivering up dozens of our agents to a gruesome fate in the Soviet Union. That still gives me a fright.

Interviewer: Nonetheless, in your thriller *Tinker, Tailor, Soldier, Spy*, you still erect a kind of memorial to him, albeit somewhat cryptic.
le Carré: We had the same background; we were given the same choice; and we reacted in a similar fashion. Both of us became entertainers, amusing people, because we craved the recognition we had been refused by our fathers. Both of us were looking for an institution to give us the integrity and guidance that we found lacking in our fathers. And both of us sought to revenge ourselves upon this institution for lack of love in childhood. Philby took the path of a criminal. I sublimated similar feelings by taking up writing. My book is a metaphor for my own disparity.

Interviewer: And so you preferred to meet with Sakharov.[1]
le Carré: You know, in a strange way Philby and Sakharov complement each other. Sakharov is the unusual example of a man who had the courage in a suppressed society to take the road of open protest; Philby, the coward, secretly revenged himself on a relatively open society. I have no doubts as to who took the right road.

---

1. Andrei Sakharov (1921–1989), Russian physicist who helped develop the Soviet hydrogen bomb but who later became an activist against the Soviet regime. He was awarded the Nobel Peace Prize in 1975.

Interviewer: Isn't Sakharov suffering from the guilt of having supplied a totalitarian state with the hydrogen bomb?

le Carré: It is difficult to imagine how somebody named Sakharov[2] can live with the knowledge of having built the bomb for a bunch of gangsters. I think the feeling of having been misguided and abused has given him the strength to put matters right. He went out into the desert, a lonely prophet, suffered the agonies of persecution. Now one would expect reconciliation, but Sakharov does not make any compromises. He never was at home in the salons of the tacticians and strategists. Why should he go there today?

Interviewer: Should the world be ruled by people like Sakharov?

le Carré: The world as a whole is safer if ruled by mediocre people.

Interviewer: In your *Russia House* there is, in a leading role, a brilliant Russian scientist who is a martyr, but also a traitor. Were there actual models for this person?

le Carré: The Penkovsky case,[3] naturally, but also Sakharov. Interestingly enough, Sakharov questioned me in great detail about the English atom spy Klaus Fuchs;[4] perhaps he was pondering if Fuchs's course of action might have been an alternative for himself.

Interviewer: The twist of your novel: the scientist does not inform the West about a new weapons system, but about an actual calamity—Russia's weaponry is a pile of scrap, the "knight dies in his armor." Has the ex-spy le Carré gained more perspicacity, of glasnost clarity?

le Carré: I have long entertained the idea that we see too much of the devil in our enemy and that we need a perestroika of our imagination. My visit to Russia has confirmed the idea: wherever I went, nothing worked, nothing functioned, and in this kind of chaos you can hardly expect the machinery of the military to give a first-rate performance, can you?

---

2. The word means *sugar* in Russian.

3. Oleg Penkovsky (1919–1963) was the highest-level Soviet official who spied for the United States.

4. Fuchs (1911–1988), a top-level physicist for both the United States and Great Britain, was revealed as a spy for the Soviet Union in 1949.

Interviewer: Now that the Cold War has ended, is there a peaceful retirement waiting for the spies of the political thriller as well?

le Carré: As long as statesmen continue to lie, states continue to compete, and mutual distrust continues to prevail, there will be espionage. For instance, it will be very exciting to see how the fragments of the crumbling "Empire of Evil" will behave. There is a heyday for mutual curiosity; whoever wants to write about it will find sufficient material.

Interviewer: So there will be a life for you after glasnost?

le Carré: The prospect is stimulating. I have been given a whole new deck of cards.

Interviewer: John le Carré, we thank you for the conversation.

Spies Who Come in From the Cold War: A Session Between John le Carré and the Soviets

Viktor Orlik / 1989

Reprinted from *World Press Review*, 36 (October 1989), pp. 28, 30–31.

From an interview with the British spy novelist John le Carré, conducted by Viktor Orlik, in the Soviet Writers Union weekly Literaturnaya Gazeta *of Moscow:*

Interviewer: It is natural to begin with the story of David Cornwell.

le Carré: I was born more than half a century ago into a bourgeois English family. My grandfather was the mayor of a small town, and his son, my father, seems to have shown a proclivity from early childhood for various sorts of adventures. By the time I came into the world, my father had to make his first acquaintance with Her Majesty's prisons for some shady financial deals. I think I realized very early that the ability to deceive and charm was one of the most reliable weapons in the arsenal for influencing the people around me.

I have a clear memory of the prewar years and British Prime Minister Neville Chamberlain's radio message to the nation in which he spoke of a coming war. At the time, we English children had a very sentimental conception of Joseph Stalin. We grew up with the feeling that the Russians were our friends, our allies. So it was a great surprise to all of us after the war that we found ourselves on different sides of the barricades. I personally found it incredible in the early 1950s, when I was serving in the British occupation army in Austria, that we were spying on the Russians. In time I learned that this espionage, which had begun in 1917 and was interrupted by the war, had essentially not stopped.

Interviewer: Your books have much to say about the Soviet people. Which of our writers do you like most?

le Carré: When I started to write my latest book, *The Russia House,* I threw myself at Russian classical literature and reread Tolstoy, Dostoyevsky, and Gogol with pleasure. I find Gogol enthralling and astonishing, although I must admit that the quality of the translations leaves something to be desired. Nevertheless, what I sensed in Russian classical literature was not only eternal themes but also the fact that these classical works are like a fragment of the socio-political and everyday life of those times.

Interviewer: Are writers, intellectuals, and creative people today capable of influencing governments or otherwise playing a more noticeable role in the struggle for the survival of mankind?

le Carré: There is an enormous difference between the respect that is accorded writers in the Soviet Union and the way our brothers are seen in the West. By and large, we in the West have a rather indifferent attitude toward writers. In the U.S.S.R., as well as in Russian history before it, the intelligentsia, writers, artists, and thinkers have held a special place in the life of society. They have a sense of high social responsibility, a need to speak for the people and to address the people. In the West, because we have a social history of expressing ourselves more openly and vociferously, writers have not performed such a public function.

At the risk of seeming immodest, I will say that when I visited the U.S. I was astonished at how attentive people were to my comments on social issues. I think this happens because basic problems are no longer the prerogative only of politicians. It seems to me that today writers in the West can play a role.

Everyone in the U.S. was interested in knowing whether what is going on in the Soviet Union is just a game, how real all of it is, and, finally, what should we do? I tried to speak about the fact that an experiment is occurring in the U.S.S.R. on gigantic scale, about how I understand *perestroika* to be a kind of return to 1917—but with greater wisdom, taking account of the Soviet Union's historical experience.

I also said that relations between the West and the Soviet Union are far from ideal, but the possibility of making them better today is a matter of our grasp and our consciences. Great and wonderful changes can take place. In the past, we tried to build relations on other principles, and it did not work. Now there is a real possibility of a great reconciliation and even a great partnership. And the role of writers here is most significant.

Interviewer: Could you clarify a delicate point regarding your work? I have in mind the "spy mania complex." Where does it come from?

le Carré: It seems to me that the obsession the British have with this subject dates to the time when the empire was being built. To maintain our power and to defend our commercial and other interests, we had to penetrate other national groups and systems and countries in order to divide and rule for the good of the British Empire. In addition, Britain's situation as an island certainly affected the English national character. We are cautious, circumspect people and quite clannish. We very quickly and easily size up each other—who you are, what you are. We also accept hypocrisy as inevitable. In other words, the sum of all of these circumstances led to a kind of national schizophrenia with regard to spy mania. In various forms, such "diseases" also afflict other nations.

We Britons are born masters of camouflage. While we have a great fondness for grand ceremonies, we are adept at carrying on our little dealings in the shadows.

Interviewer: In *The Looking-Glass War*, one of your earlier books, the people engaged in espionage look like children who have not grown up or adults who have reverted to childhood. Is that the case?

le Carré: Yes. I will venture an opinion that will displease many people: Such activities often attract immature, undeveloped people who have broken away from their anchor and are seeking "absolute" answers to their personal problems. The paradox is that those who get involved in these seemingly heroic activities are often narrow-minded and rather helpless people who fancy that they know more than ordinary mortals and that they are better than others because they have a gun in their pockets. The psychology of being part of an exclusive group justifies any not-very-clean business, any cheap lie, any wickedness that is supposedly undertaken in the name of some higher interest. There is a well-known English saying that a diplomat is a gentleman who lies for the good of his country. Deception, unfortunately, is largely a self-reproducing way of life in these organizations.

For all that, however, it is not enough to say that these organizations are necessary. Strange as it may seem, they perform vitally important functions. We must know about each other; we must be able to observe each other. These organizations are an expression of necessary distrust that will always exist. It is another matter that they should be more decent in the future and serve us rather than themselves. I found it to be very appropriate and timely that the new head of the KGB said—I don't know to what extent it squares with reality—that their work will be based precisely on these principles. But one must bear in mind that we created these organizations, and disbanding them would be practically impossible. Many organizations engage in shadowing, surveillance, and observation. They are difficult to dismantle, but we should not give up attempts to do so.

Interviewer: Can the secret services play a positive role in relations between nations by helping to decrease the risk of war?
le Carré: To begin with, I should say that the intelligence agencies are, in a sense, acting on behalf of rival arms producers—a point I make in my latest book.[1] We are thereby attesting, in effect, to the futility and senselessness of the idea of a first nuclear strike. But that is not enough. Mikhail Gorbachev's nearly unilateral initiatives in this respect caught us by surprise; we did not have a contingency plan in the event of an end to the Cold War, nor did we have a plan in case peace broke out. So the inertia of old approaches persists, although we really would like to live and act in a new way.

I have tried to dramatize and expose this contradiction, this danger, by writing about the activities of the secret services. In real life, I think, the intelligence agencies can oversee compliance with arms-control agreements that have already been concluded, as well as with new ones that I hope will soon be signed. Let them expend their energy for these purposes. But the main point is that the intelligence agencies, in their methods, forms, and the essence of their activities, should reflect the changes that our times are bringing about.

Interviewer: In *The Russia House*, one senses a hope of improvements in East-West relations.
le Carré: I think everything looks more fascinating and exciting in real life. Gorbachev has awakened in the world—maybe even more in the West than in the Soviet Union—what I would call hope and impatience. For more than forty years, we have lived under the burden of a horrifying threat to our children and grandchildren—not to mention to ourselves. There was a time—happily, it is being erased from our memories—when month after month we

1. *The Russia House.*

would be surprised to discover that we were still living in the shadow of an unabating nuclear threat. Gorbachev's message is universal. He is addressing those who command influence and authority in the world and those who remember the four decades of the Cold War, who remember the difficult and bitter years of the Soviet Union's history, the tragedy of Stalinism, the great expectations of the Khrushchev era, and the disillusionments that came with the Brezhnev period. We are "thawing out," becoming free people.

My last, beautiful love is *glasnost* and *perestroika*. I must say that all of this has become, in the most extraordinary way, a psychological possession for a great many people outside the Soviet Union. I happened to be in New York when Gorbachev addressed the United Nations, and it was precisely his idealism that filled the vacuum left over after the routine U.S. presidential election.[2] He was the one who spoke on behalf of humanity, who effectively handed to the starving the bread of hope. I am convinced that this is the beginning of a spiritual and positive revolution in politics.

Some may say that this is overstated. No, it is not. We have indulged for too long in negativism, hostility, and chauvinism. We have preferred the weaker, corrupted forms of patriotism, which replaced religion for us on both sides of the Iron Curtain. Today we are witnessing the emergence of new opportunities. The point is not the individual changes. The point is that for the first time in my life I have felt that, together, we can change the way people think.

Mass attitudes are beginning to prod political change. West German Chancellor Helmut Kohl[3] is compelled to take greater account of public opinion. Prime Minister Margaret Thatcher is discovering that she can no longer portray Britain as a nation that is surrounded by enemies from the continent and that lives under a constant threat from the Russian bear. This no longer works. It seems to me that something similar is also taking place in the U.S. I hope that people in the Soviet Union also have these feelings, since Gorbachev came to us as a leader who set in motion processes that are unstoppable. I am firmly convinced of this.

Interviewer: Do you regard today's changing Soviet Union as an "enemy" of the West?

2. Gorbachev addressed the United Nations in December 1988, following the landslide victory of Republican George Herbert Walker Bush over Democrat Michael Dukakis in the November election.
3. Kohl served as German Chancellor from 1982 to 1998.

le Carré: I think that remnants of hostility will remain in both blocs for quite a long time. It would be naive to presume that we could sweep all of this away with one stroke, and it seems to me that both superpowers are still somewhat frightened by the notion of how they will live without an "enemy image." The politician's traditional method, when his country is endangered by internal difficulties, contradictions, and conflicts, is to designate an external enemy.

I personally have the greatest respect and admiration for the fact that, in the face of ethnic, social, and economic problems, Gorbachev did not go down that path. He rejects the psychology of the besieged fortress, and in this respect he is ahead of the U.S. The danger—and history has repeatedly confirmed this—is that when you need an enemy, you don't stop looking until you find one. The fact that Gorbachev rejects this seems to me one of the most astonishing and impressive traits of your leader.

I would like to end by saying that it is you who are leading in the race to eliminate the enemy image. It is a brilliant diplomatic initiative, which excites and thrills the imagination of mankind.

We Distorted Our Own Minds

Walter Isaacson and James Kelly / 1993

Interviewer: If you were the director of the CIA, what priorities would you set for the next decade?

le Carré: What I would require of my intelligence service would be a real liaison with major existing intelligence services on shared targets. That would include terrorism and nuclear weapons, all these loose cannons we've got sloshing around in Ukraine. If some crazed national movement got hold of nuclear weapons, then I think there should be a joint effort among intelligence agencies that should be pooled by the United Nations.

Interviewer: Won't countries be reluctant to share intelligence data with one another through the U.N.?

le Carré: Those are barriers which somehow or another have to be dismantled. Those are our Cold War manners. Of course, all intelligence services like to retain their mystique. The first thing the Americans do if they get a wonderful report from the Israelis is edit it, retitle it, put all sorts of stamps all over it and shove it upstairs. This is another reason, incidentally, why intelligence assessments are so frequently distorted: the same source can fund a whole lot of seemingly separate intelligence documents. Let's say, the Israelis prepare a document which they're prepared to give to an American liaison. They're also prepared to give another version of this same intelligence to the French. The French receive it and immediately signal some of it for economic gain to the Syrians. Then the National Security Agency comes in, intercepts France to Damascus, and there you get corroboration of the intelligence which has already come through from the same source. It's the proof cooked three different ways, but has actually come from the same source.

Interviewer: Intelligence gathering by human spies is now coming back into vogue. Wouldn't that be far more effective than satellites in a place like Somalia?

le Carré: That would be great, but you've really got to buy somebody who is there. You've got to deal through intermediaries you know. You're going through a whole ladder of contacts—you end up sending a gold vase to a motel on the road to Mogadishu—you never see the gold vase again—you never get any intelligence. It requires a street wisdom suddenly in a particular area which is terribly hard for an intelligence service to produce when the President suddenly says, "Get me that damned warlord."

Interviewer: One of the great intelligence debacles of the Cold War was the overestimation of the Soviet Union's capabilities. How did that happen?
le Carré: I think it was a failure of intelligence and, in a curious way, a failure of common sense. The overkill of coverage was so immense that they literally started counting the cows twice, that when you have huge amounts of data coming in, it's very easy to lose count as simply as that. But the failure of common sense is absolutely weird in its stupidity. Any good journalist who'd been living in Moscow in the later years of Brezhnev would know that nothing worked anymore. The knight was dying inside his armor, and somehow that human perception never made itself felt in intelligence analyses.

Interviewer: Is there something inherent about spying that causes spies not to see the bigger picture?
le Carré: Absolutely. If you live in secrecy, you think in secrecy. It is the very nature of the life you lead as an intelligence officer in a secret room that the ordinary winds of common sense don't blow through it. You are constantly looking to relate to your enemy in intellectual, adversarial and conspiratorial terms. It is absolutely necessary to the intelligence mentality that you put the worst interpretation upon your adversary.

Interviewer: Did our obsession with secrecy hurt our own governments?
le Carré: I believe that's exactly what we did to ourselves. We really did entrench anticommunism and enforce it in ways that in my view were catastrophic. We distorted our own minds; it was almost a precursor of political correctness in its worst form.

Interviewer: *Catastrophic* is a pretty strong word.
le Carré: It is a strong word. The post-Cold War trauma that we identify in the former Soviet Union, perhaps less dramatically and less scarily, is among

us too. We've had removed from us a system of priorities in thinking and responding which has left us for the moment rather inarticulate and undirected in our collective thinking. We have squandered the peace that we've won with the Cold War. We had some kind of vision in the Cold War; we got a crusade going even when we were mistaken and crude about it.

I think there was never a time when we needed rhetoric so badly, when we needed a new romantic dream. I see at the moment, and I hope it's only an intervening moment in our world history, a time of absolute moral failure by the West to perceive its own role in the future. Since we have now contrived to unscrew the binding shackles of communism, I think we have to be ready to pick up the bits, and I think we have to be ready fairly often to respond extremely quickly to brush-fire wars and things of that sort.

Interviewer: In the end, was Cold War espionage counterproductive or productive in helping us preserve our national security?
le Carré: If I had to cast a stone into one bucket or the other, I would say it was counterproductive. Now if we had been angels, if we had been superwise, we would have realized that our resources would have been much better deployed showing ourselves to be constitutionally impeccable and not worrying about the few traitors and fewer spies you inevitably let through the net. It was a war that had to be fought, but it was not the war that won the whole campaign. Indeed, what espionage looks like now is what it always was: a sideshow got up as major theater.

Where I kick myself is where I think I actually contributed to the myth of the intelligence services as being very good. When I wrote *The Spy Who Came in From the Cold*, the head of operations at the Secret Intelligence Service remarked that it was the only bloody double agent that ever worked. The mythmaking that went on all around us contributed to the kind of ingrown and corrosive self-perceptions that were at the heart of our undoing.

Interviewer: You worked in a British intelligence as a young man. How do you look back upon those years now?
le Carré: I was recruited almost when I was still in diapers into that world. My really formative years, the years when one should be having nice little love affairs and doing different jobs and finding out who one shouldn't be and that stuff, they were all taken over by the secret world. The moods that I remember, the self-perceptions I had, were very positive, very negative; I was

brilliant, I was a complete idiot. I entered it in the spirit of John Buchan and left it in the spirit of Kafka.

Interviewer: Was there a particular incident that formed your view of espionage?

le Carré: I remember one episode where I was obliged to interrogate a British official about his alleged involvement in an espionage ring, and he lied to me. He just lied all the way through. I made a very reasoned submission to my superiors and went on to other things and discovered to my astonishment a few months later, this man had been promoted. So I was terribly worried, and I started to shake the bars. Finally I was taken aside and told to ask no more questions about the matter. And of course years later I realized that he had been our man, our informant, inside the ring that we had penetrated. Therefore I was actually simply part of his cover story. All they wanted me to do was rubber-stamp him so he could get on with his life again.

Interviewer: How do you ensure that the spies remain honest brokers of intelligence and don't try to distort it for their own ends?

le Carré: What we've seen again and again, when there's been a Watergate or there's been something else, is this curious mixture that includes the real zealots who believe they can repair the inadequacies of the democratic system by doing unofficial things. They think they're the heroes. Then you see the total misfits who need to take shelter in secret rooms and who actually get off being secretive.

It is actually only very excited, over-stimulated men on very short sleep, together with all the toys of supersecrecy and the helicopters and the special passes, that inevitably produce irrational behavior. But those people, when they began, were ordinary guys; they were like us. Nöel Annan, who was in British intelligence for years, said nobody should be allowed to do it more than three years, that one way of keeping an intelligence service sane is to have it run entirely by temporary people.

Interviewer: When the Cold War ended, did you feel any nostalgia?

le Carré: I didn't have nostalgia, but I went through some of the trauma that the spooks had definitely been through. Was there nothing there? Maybe it was all a waste of life. Maybe I should have just been running a boy's club. I had this weird kind of sub-life in some part of my head, where I sort of kept up with events from a spy's-eye view. I was never a very good spook; I was definitely a writer who took up spying rather than a spy who took up writing.

Interviewer: So you were happy to see the Cold War end. . . .
le Carré: Yeah, I was thrilled. Part of my present indignation is that I want the world to be a better place now. I think the Americans have the energy and the record and the right to conduct the altruistic crusade. I think it's totally incorrect politically to suggest it, but a new period of altruistic white colonialism is upon us.

Interviewer: Pax Americana Moralistica?
le Carré: Yes, a little bit, although I don't think it need be as expansive as we fear. I don't see you sort of ferrying your armed police all over the world keeping order. I think it's much more how you throw your weight in the world arena politically, and how you demonstrate your outrage at flagrant misbehavior in places where it can be stopped.

Remarks to the Knopf Sales Force

John le Carré / 1996

Reprinted from a promotional piece, 12 August 1996.

Let me tell you a few things about myself. Not much, but enough. In the old days it was convenient to bill me as a spy turned writer. I was nothing of the kind. I am a writer who, when I was very young, spent a few ineffectual but extremely formative years in British Intelligence.

I never knew my mother till I was twenty-one. I act like a gent but I am wonderfully badly born. My father was a confidence trickster and a gaol bird. Read *A Perfect Spy*.

I hate the telephone. I can't type. Like the tailor in my new novel,[1] I ply my trade by hand. I live on a Cornish cliff and hate cities. Three days and nights in a city are about my maximum. I don't see many people. I write and walk and swim and drink.

Apart from spying, I have in my time sold bathtowels, got divorced, washed elephants, run away from school, decimated a flock of Welsh sheep with a twenty-five-pound shell because I was too stupid to understand the gunnery officer's instructions, taught the sons of the rich at Eton College, and backward children in a special school.

I have four sons and ten grandchildren. It is well over thirty years since I hung up my cloak and dagger. I wrote my first three books while I was a spook, I wrote the next thirteen after I was at large.

If I had gone to sea instead going to the spies, I would have written about the sea. Joseph Conrad did that, and used the seafaring life superbly as his theatre of man's striving, with its own laws and language and morality, its own cruelties and rewards and glimpses of the infinite.

Sometimes Conrad used the sea to scare the pants off us. Sometimes to tell us a love story. Or a comedy.

And as a cat may look at a king, I look to Conrad for that example— except that, by an accident of life, the mast that I served before was the secret one. Spying—not the sea—became my element.

---

1. *The Tailor of Panama.*

And when a writer has found his element, there is no limit to the stories he can tell, except that limit imposed by his own creative talent.

I wonder how Joseph Conrad would have fared on the *Today* show:

- "Joe, is the Polish Navy today superior to the American Navy?"
- "Joe, what are your views, please, on same-sex relationships below decks?"
- "Joe, how do you regard the expansion of the motorised yacht industry as applied to your writings?"

A good writer is an expert on nothing except himself. And on that subject, if he is wise, he holds his tongue. Some of you may wonder why I am reluctant to submit to interviews on television and radio and in the press.

The answer is that *nothing* I write is authentic. It is the stuff of dreams, not reality. Yet I am treated by the media as though I wrote espionage handbooks. I am regarded as a sage on every spy case from the double-agent Judas to your wretched Mr. Aldrich Ames.[2]

And to a point I am flattered that my fabulations are taken so seriously. Yet I also despise myself in the fake role of guru, since it bears no relation to who I am or what I do. Artists, in my experience, have very little centre. They fake. They are not the real thing. They are spies. I am no exception.

Which brings me—a little more naturally than I care to think—to the case of Harry Pendel, of the House of Pendel & Braithwaite Co. Limitada, Tailors to Royalty, Panama.

The Tailor of Panama is a spy story, it has a beginning, a middle and an end, it has characters I love, and I immodestly believe it is what I intended it to be: savage, satirical, sad, funny, exciting and extremely entertaining.

And my tailor Harry Pendel is an artist. He likes to give style and form to people who have none of their own. He dresses the world as he wishes to see it, not as it is. And he touches it with magic.

Because he's a little guy with big dreams. Because he has done some prison. And because he knows that the world can be a pretty cruel place.

He's an artist, but not of the confrontational kind: an escape artist, an avoider, a fabulist. Yet full of kindliness, and with his own strange brand of decency.

2. CIA official who was a Soviet mole; he was arrested in 1994.

And because he has a past, and because nothing goes away in life, he finds himself saddled with the impossible job of spying for his country.

So Harry Pendel does what any of us might do, but it's also what he does for a living, and it's the only skill he possesses: he starts to dress things up. Invent. Dream. Fabricate.

And in doing so, he tells his spymasters what they want to hear. And they in turn add a tuck here and a pull there, so that *their* masters also hear what they want to hear: a thing that happens every day everywhere, whether in the world of spying or politics or media reporting, or for that matter publishing.

Truth is what people want to hear. Secrets are what you tell one person at a time.

And what results from Harry Pendel's fabrications is something I hope you will read for yourselves. And I hope that as you laugh a little and shudder a little, and turn the pages, you will recognise in the secret world of Harry Pendel things that belong in the everybody's world.

The book is written for you, and for me, and for everybody who has known what it is to live under corporate disciplines, to suffer the folly of superiors, and to struggle to survive in a world that very often seems to be going seriously mad.

Do you know something? It's August 12th. Today, thirty-five years ago, the Berlin Wall went up. I was there. The British Prime Minister Harold Macmillian received the news on a Scottish grouse moor because August 12th is by tradition the first day of grouse shooting. He told the journalists it was all got up by the press and went on shooting grouse. And I hurried home and wrote *The Spy Who Came in From the Cold*.

I did a lot of hard labour after that and life wasn't always easy and the books weren't all perfect. But I also had a lot of fun.

And I hope that you can share, with the publication of this book, some of the fun I had in writing of it, and some of the affection I feel for the characters.

Master of the Secret World: John le Carré on Deception, Storytelling and American Hubris

Andrew Ross / 1996

John le Carré says he would like to get a few more novels under his belt. Then one day, at the appropriate time, he imagines that someone will appear behind him, hammer at the ready, who will say, "Okay, that's enough." If his latest novel, his sixteenth since 1961, is any indication, that day remains far off.

In The Tailor of Panama, *le Carré, at age sixty-five, exhibits an energy that critics feared he had lost with the passing of the Cold War. He also shows a previously unheralded knack for pure farce. At least, le Carré says, he hasn't plunged his friends into depression this time. Which doesn't mean that he has lost his cold moral vision, nor the internal demons that drive him to write.*

We talked with le Carré during a brief stopover in Los Angeles, where he was visiting two of his sons and assorted grandchildren.

Interviewer: In your acknowledgments, you say this book would not have been written had it not been for Graham Greene's *Our Man in Havana*. Greene subtitled his book "An Entertainment," not a word usually associated with le Carré. If you had to put a label on *The Tailor of Panama*, what would it be?

le Carré: Greene was ill-advised to categorize his own work. I think that is a job for the literary bureaucracy and not for the writer. But if I had to put a name to it, I would wish that all my books were entertainments. I think the first thing you've got to do is grab the reader by the ear, and make him sit down and listen. Make him laugh, make him feel. We all want to be entertained at a very high level. That is the beginning of the relationship, the symbiosis between the writer and the reader.

Interviewer: Still, the antic, comic elements in *The Tailor of Panama* will come as a surprise to many of your readers. You certainly seem to be in a lighter mood here.

le Carré: I think I'm in the same mood as ever, but in some ways more mature. I guess you could say that, at sixty-five, when you've seen the world shape up as I have, there are only two things you can do: laugh or kill yourself. I think my leading character effectively does both.

Interviewer: That world is certainly present in the book, but you also deeply and passionately explore character, as well as external events, this time.

le Carré: In some ways it's a very personal book. I was exploring the relationship between myself and my own fabricator. Anybody in the creative business, as you might call it, has some sense of guilt about fooling around with fact, that you're committing larceny, that all of life is material for your fabulations. That was certainly Harry Pendel's position. So I found some kind of buzz running between me and the main character, which I had not really felt since *A Perfect Spy.*

Interviewer: Pendel's ability to create worlds out of whole cloth, as you write, was necessary to fill major gaps in his psyche. It was also ultimately destructive to himself and the people he loved best. Do you feel some of those gaps yourself?

le Carré: Yes, I suppose I do feel some of those gaps myself. What Harry did is, in a sense, merely an exaggeration of what we all do to coexist. We lie to one another every day, in the sweetest way, often unconsciously. We dissemble—"Yes, darling, I'm fine." We dress ourselves and compose ourselves in order to present ourselves to one another.

Now Pendel took that a little far. But people who've had very unhappy childhoods are pretty good at inventing themselves. If nobody invents you for yourself, nothing is left but to invent yourself for others. It became destructive in Harry's case when his "gift" was put to political use, until, in a sense, too much was asked of him. It's rather like an artist whose bluff is called.

Interviewer: You mentioned *A Perfect Spy*, which you've said was really about your own father, a con man. Are there shades of your father again in this book?

le Carré: Yes, in Uncle Benny, in the criminal background, and the fun that Uncle Benny was. They are like the court of people who frequented my father's house. He loved all those immigrants, all those striving guys from different walks of life, whether they were criminal or not.

Interviewer: Uncle Benny is Jewish, from the East End of London. Did you have any fears, in tackling Jewish characters and using their vernacular, that people might say you were embracing anti-Semitic stereotypes?
le Carré: I have carried that label around with me ever since I wrote *The Little Drummer Girl*. I received such awful letters from organized Jewish groups that I never felt on safe ground after that. My great sin was suggesting that the state of Israel—that Palestine—was in fact a twice-promised land.

Still, I didn't feel queasy about addressing the tradition of Jewish tailors in the East End. It's so deeply embedded, and so historically extended, that most of the good jokes are true. There *was* a community of rascally Jewish tailors. The insurance companies, many of which were Jewish, referred to "Jewish lightning" when unfortunate fires burned down warehouses in the East End. It was a period when Jews from the ghettos and the *shtetls* of Eastern Europe set up their own sweatshops in London, and terribly exploited their own families, necessarily perhaps, in order to undercut the cost of mass manufacture. They lived in wretched circumstances, fighting bare-knuckled in the streets, and always the underdog—as every ethnic community moving into the East End of London has been. It is just a chunk of history. There were a lot of old, Jewish tailors who had wonderful tales to tell, most of them far more rascally than I dared to relate in the book.

Interviewer: Apart from Graham Greene, there were hints of Evelyn Waugh, especially *Scoop*.
le Carré: You haven't mentioned P. G. Wodehouse. I would like to think that the master was in there somewhere. I don't think I consciously reach for any of that stuff, but they're part of literary memory; they're what's in the pot.

Interviewer: In the "Personal Best" essay you wrote for *Salon*, you described Ford Madox Ford's *The Good Soldier* as one of the finest, though neglected, novels of the twentieth century. That was also a story about deceit, which you return to time and time again. How much of an influence was Ford on your writing?
le Carré: It was the solitude of the deceit and the pity with which Ford described the deceiver. In an extreme case that is the condition in which all of

us live in some ways: The longing we have to communicate cleanly and directly with people is always obstructed by qualifications and often with concern about how our messages will be received—whether we will lose face because those messages will be received untruthfully. In *The Good Soldier*, it seemed to me that Edward Ashburnham was really a decently-motivated victim of deceit.

Interviewer: Like Alec Leamas (*The Spy Who Came in From the Cold*), Jerry Westerby (*The Honorable Schoolboy*), Harry Pendel. Even George Smiley—
le Carré: Remember Graham Greene's dictum that childhood is the bank balance of the writer. I think that all writers feel alienated. Most of us go back to an alienated childhood in some way or another. I know that I do. That is the crucible really. By the age of nine or ten, I knew, like Harry Pendel, that I had to cut my own cloth and make my own way. Harry felt the lash; all the circumstances in his life compounded to make him a man who looked inward rather than outward. He really believes he's responsible for the whole world because it is he who doesn't fit in with it.

Interviewer: Sixteen novels later, do you still feel that way?
le Carré: Yes, I think I do. Of course you get craftier with writing; and, probably, once you're comfortable with a perspective upon life, you go back to certain situations and work them. I am at a stage in my life—now quite late—where I am completely reconciled to what I am as a writer. I know what I can and can't do. I love writing. I feel it is my best time. But I still feel, as I think most creative people do, absolutely isolated. And, as Pendel does, I am still making order out of chaos by reinvention. I suppose I had a more orga-nized sense of chaos as I approached this story than I have had before, and therefore a greater urgency to tell it.

Interviewer: Are you more reconciled to the outer workings of the world, or at least the spy world?
le Carré: There are some perceptions I feel I have now that I didn't have before. One of them relates to the difference between experience and news. In every war zone that I've been in, there has been a reality and then there has been the public perception of why the war was being fought. In every crisis, in every confrontation that has come my way, the issues have been far more complex than the public has been allowed to know.

Take the simple issue of "Operation Just Cause."[1] Simple—ha, ha—when George Bush, to get away from the "wimp factor," launched an invasion against a client state of the CIA because the CIA's former agent,[2] had run amok. Add to that the question of whether the treaty between Jimmy Carter and Omar Torrijos[3] was really going to be honored by the Americans in the future. Add to that again the increasing Japanese influence in the region, which was at that time a matter of great concern to the U.S. Finally, add the concerns of big American corporations who wanted to invest vastly in the two ports at either end of the canal. What you get is a story infinitely more complex than the U.S. having to go in and quell a madman who had the temerity to have his troops beat up American women in the streets.

Interviewer: You differentiate between news and experience, but a lot of your readers think they may be getting the straight news—especially about intelligence agencies—when the fact is you are making up characters and situations. Have we taken your books a little too seriously?
le Carré: Yes, I am quite sure that's the case. I have to accept it as a compliment, of course, because every writer wants to be believed. But every writer knows he is spurious; every fiction writer would rather be credible than authentic.

Interviewer: What's the difference?
le Carré: Authentic is non-fiction, the reality. My stories have to resolve themselves. There has to be a beginning, a middle and an end. In the authentic world, almost no espionage case is ever resolved, because you don't want it to be resolved. You want the man or the woman to stay in place, to continue working for you. If he or she loses her effectiveness, you fade the person out and life goes on. Now, that doesn't make a story—that's "the cat sat on the mat." I have to tell "the cat sat on the dog's mat." I have to produce the tension, the danger, and so on. The disciplines of storytelling require that I shape, out of the monotony and everyday life of espionage, something that has a beginning, a middle and an end. That's already contrary to the reality.

---

1. The December 1989 U.S. effort to end Manuel Noriega's regime (1983–1989) and establish a U.S.-recognized government in Panama.
2. Noriega.
3. Panamanian leader, 1968–1978; in an agreement signed by Carter and Torrijos, the United States committed to surrender control of the Panama Canal to Panama by December 31, 1999.

Then, I have to introduce levels of intelligence on both sides and in each protagonist, which very probably do not pertain. I have to introduce levels of moral doubt, self-doubt, which may not pertain. I mean a guy who just takes ten thousand bucks to go and do something probably is not asking whether he can reconcile this to his maker. But in my books, he has to.

So I use the furniture of espionage to amuse the reader, to make the reader listen to me, because most people like to read about intrigue and spies. I hope to provide a metaphor for the average reader's daily life. Most of us live in a slightly conspiratorial relationship with our employer and perhaps with our marriage. I think what gives my works whatever universality they have is that they use the metaphysical secret world to describe some realities of the overt world.

Interviewer: You actually invented espionage jargon.
le Carré: Spies tell me that it's now entered their language! It's been more than forty years since I had anything to do with the secret world. But as I've gone on writing I've really just refined the uses of that world as my private theater. Added and subtracted and changed it, tried to make it reflect the mood of the day.

Interviewer: How does that play out in *The Tailor of Panama*?
le Carré: In the story we have somebody working for an entirely corrupt British institution who is soliciting intelligence which is fabricated. We don't know if he knows it's fabricated. We do know this: as far as he's concerned, *it plays upstairs*, they like it in the board room, so he lets it ride. In the board room they're already re-writing it because they want to serve it up to the politicos and their customers and to the people who finance the secret service. So we've got at every level, cost effectiveness, price consciousness and privatization—all these extolled virtues that Mrs. Thatcher so admired in Reaganomics and imported into Britain. In my story, we've got them running wild, which seems to me to be a metaphor for our time.

Interviewer: You don't paint a very pretty picture of "Operation Just Cause."
le Carré: Bush's invasion of Panama in the end was probably necessary, and it was certainly successful. But, as Richard Koster[4] said, the United States performed a brilliant piece of surgery for lung cancer on a patient to whom it had

4. American novelist residing in Panama.

been providing cigarettes for the last thirty years. By using it as a training base, as a place for conducting wars against perceived rebels and communists, as some kind of launching pad against Castro for intelligence purposes, and getting very mixed up in the drugs trade. There is a story—true or not, but I suspect it is true—that as part of the deal with Noriega, the CIA turned a blind eye to the flow of large quantities of cocaine into California in return for guns and arms to the Contras. It may be true. It certainly was true in Southeast Asia. I saw that on the ground.

Interviewer: The term "blowback"—as we're seeing with the fundamentalist Muslims we armed in Afghanistan—comes to mind.
le Carré: It was inevitable. Americans are "get up and go" by nature; they believe that if you know something, you should do something about it. But when you apply that to an intelligence service—taking sides, arming groups, and so on—you really are operating on a pretty dangerous basis. Everything has its consequences in this business. Nothing goes away. The deals and the promises that you make today really do come home to roost. The more secrets, sometimes, the more violent the response.

Interviewer: Again, speaking of news and experience, your portrayal of the press is pretty unflattering.
le Carré: In the last fifteen or twenty years, I've watched the British press simply go to hell. There seems to be no limit, no depths to which the tabloids won't sink. I don't know who these people are but they're little pigs. Even with the "quality" papers, the standard of literacy is pathetic. Journalists pipe their stories right into the paper, and nobody really has time even to correct the spelling.

When Rupert Murdoch[5] took over a great chunk of the British press, the remaining newspapers had a choice whether to go up-market or down-market. Because it is the custom of people in the entertainment and information business to underrate the public, they selected, almost to a man, the downward route. Fabrication by a journalist—the story too good to check out—is almost par for the course. I've ceased to give interviews in Britain, having read that I was in the habit of frequenting a guru in India. In my entire life I've spent but three days in India. Never in my life have I spoken to any guru.

---

5. Australian-born media mogul.

Interviewer: We haven't seen a le Carré book on the big screen, or small, since *The Russia House*. Why not?

le Carré: We should have seen *The Night Manager* by now. Paramount paid a great fortune for it. For some reason it simply fell into some kind of hole. Sydney Pollack was supposed to have directed it. He's gone on to something else. Robert Towne was supposed to have written it. Whatever he wrote was, shall we say, not held to be satisfactory. To say any more would get me straight into a libel court. I hope that we shall see a movie of *Our Game*, but until there is some kind of studio announcement, I shouldn't get into it. I'm getting mating signals on *The Tailor of Panama* from the industry, but nothing signed.

Interviewer: Almost like clockwork you produce a new book every two years. Are you already thinking about your next one?

le Carré: This one went so quickly. I was still correcting proofs seven weeks ago. I haven't had much time to think, but yes, I have an idea of where I would go. When you're my age and you see a story, you better go for it pretty quickly. I'd just like to get a few more novels under my belt. Then I'd like to have somebody standing behind me with a hammer who says, "Okay, that's enough." Thank heaven, though, one of the few mistakes I haven't made is to talk about the unwritten book.

Interviewer: I hear that you have joined the computer age, albeit with trepidation.

le Carré: We have an extra telephone line installed and we have a Mac. I think by Christmas we'll be all set up and ready to go. It's my wife, Jane, who will actually sit at the controls. I am moving gradually towards it. I accept that it is quite impossible to stand aside from it. I happen to write by hand. I don't even type. I'll have to change my spots.

Interviewer: le Carré goes online?

le Carré: It's going to help enormously at the most elementary level of research. I'm really a library man, or second-hand book man. In the past I have had to pay out a lot of money to get BBC monitoring service reports and that stuff. It's all been a laborious business. The notion that we can really plug into huge amounts of data, which could be interesting, is really wonderful. Of course I've come to it late, but one does, eventually.

Interviewer: Of your sixteen novels, where would you fit *The Tailor of Panama*?

le Carré: I think the ones I want to be buried with are *A Perfect Spy* and this one. I have the most affection for the characters in those stories, and somehow, they came the closest to the bone. By closest to the bone I mean as near as I want to come to my own center, the most intimate and personal to myself. And the laughs. It's wonderful to meet one's friends after they've read *The Tailor of Panama* and find them grinning all over their faces for a change, instead of being plunged into depression.

John le Carré: The Art of Fiction

George Plimpton / 1997

Reprinted from the *Paris Review*, 39 (Summer 1997), pp. 50–74. Copyright © 1997 the *Paris Review*. Reprinted by permission of Regal Literary as agent for the *Paris Review*.

The interview took place in the auditorium of New York's YHMA on a late autumn day in 1996. le Carré had arrived from London earlier that day to promote the publication of his sixteenth novel, The Tailor of Panama. *The auditorium was packed. After the interview he cheerfully submitted to questioning by the crowd, then moved to an adjoining space where autograph-seekers, some carrying more than a dozen books, had formed a long queue that curled around the room. le Carré, who likes to turn in early, looked fatigued. He stayed on until almost midnight, ministering to each request in a broad, legible hand.*

Interviewer: Can you say something about your early reading?

le Carré: I grew up in a completely bookless household. It was my father's boast that he had never read a book from end to end. I don't remember any of his ladies being bookish. So I was entirely dependent on my schoolteachers for my early reading with the exception of *The Wind in the Willows*, which a stepmother read to me when I was in hospital. My earliest reading included Maugham, the heroic English storytellers, Henty, Sapper, Peter Cheyney[1] and, thank heaven, the great and wonderful Conan Doyle. I graduated joyously to Dickens and erratically to Bernard Shaw and Galsworthy. And cautiously to the heavy contemporaries, Koestler, Gide and Camus. But the big explosion in my reading occurred in my late teens when I was seduced by the German muse. I devoured the whole of German literature alive, as it seems to me now. I have probably read more German literature than I have English. Today my pleasure is with nineteenth-century storytellers: Balzac, Dickens and the rest.

---

1. G. A. Henty (1832–1902) wrote historical novels for boys; Sapper was the pen-name for H. C. McNeile (1888–1937) who wrote fiction about crime and war; Peter Cheyney (d. 1951) wrote crime novels.

Interviewer: And among contemporary writers?

le Carré: Everything by Marquez, and sudden batches of new writers. Most recently, practically everything by Beryl Bainbridge, just for the pleasure of her ear. I read most between books, and very little fiction while I am writing.

Interviewer: You taught at Eton for a while. What did you teach, and was your stay there of any value to your writing?

le Carré: I taught principally German language and literature at Eton. But any master with private pupils must be prepared to teach anything they ask for. That can be as diverse as the early paintings of Salvador Dali or how bumble-bees manage to fly. Eton is a place of extremes, and these were good for me as a writer. The English upper classes can be seen at their best and worst. The good pupils are often brilliant, and they keep you on your toes and take you to the limits of your knowledge. The worst pupils provide a unique insight into the criminal mind. On all these counts my time at Eton provided me with riches. I even set one early novel in a school that was quite like Eton: *A Murder of Quality*.

Interviewer: Why did you change your name?

le Carré: When I began writing, I was what was politely called "a foreign servant." I went to my employers and said that I'd written my first novel. They read it and said they had no objections, but even if it were about butterflies, they said, I would have to choose a pseudonym. So then I went to my publisher, Victor Gollancz, who was Polish by origin, and he said, "My advice to you, old fellow, is to choose a good Anglo-Saxon couple of syllables. Mono-syllables." He suggested something like Chunk-Smith. So as is my courteous way, I promised to be Chunk-Smith. After that, memory eludes me and the lie takes over. I was asked so many times why I chose this ridiculous name; then the writer's imagination came to my help. I saw myself riding over Battersea Bridge, on top of a bus, looking down at a tailor's shop. Funnily enough, it *was* a tailor's shop, because I had a terrible obsession about buying clothes in order to become a diplomat in Bonn. And it *was* called something of this sort—le Carré. That satisfied everybody for years. But lies don't last with age. I find a frightful compulsion towards truth these days. And the truth is, I don't know.

Interviewer: Which intelligence service were you in?

le Carré: Even now, some residual sense of loyalty prevents me from talking much about it. I entered the secret world when I was young. I kind of lurched into it. There never seemed an alternative. I was first picked up when I was a young student in Bern, having run away from my first school. I retained what is politely called "a reporting responsibility." Then, for my military service, I went to Austria. That was a very formative time, because one of my jobs was trolling through the displaced-persons camps, looking for people who were fake refugees, or for people whose circumstances were so attractive to us from an intelligence point of view that we might consider returning them, with their consent, to the countries they came from. For a person of, as I was then, barely twenty-one, it was an immense responsibility at an extraordinary moment in history, which, horrible as it was, I was very pleased to have shared. Afterwards, after teaching at Eton, I went into the Cold-War setup properly. In all I don't suppose that I spooked around for more than seven or eight years, and that's forty years ago, but that was my little university for the purposes that I needed later to write. I think that if I'd gone to sea at that time I would have written about the sea. If I'd gone into advertising or stockbroking, that would have been my stuff. It was from there that I began abstracting and peopling my other world, my alternative, private world, which became my patch, and it became a Tolkien-like operation, except that none of my characters have hair between their toes.

Interviewer: Was there a moment during all of this when you really felt that you were going to write about it?

le Carré: There was. I had the curious and very rewarding example when I was in the first of the two services that I joined of working with a man called John Bingham, whose real name was Lord Clanmorris.[2] He was a thriller writer, and also an extremely good intelligence officer, a moleish, tubby fellow. He gave me not only the urge to write, but also a kind of outline of George Smiley, which I later filled in from other sources, notably my own. He and a don at Oxford whom I knew very well became parts of this composite character called Smiley.

2. John Bingham (1908–1988). Cornwell discussed their friendship and break in his introduction to the reprint of Bingham's *Five Roundabouts to Heaven* (London: Pan, 2000): "As far as he was concerned, I had repaid him by betraying everything outside his family that he held most dear in the world: his country, his Service, his colleagues, the bond he shared with his agents in the field, and by extension his own humanity."

Interviewer: Did you find it easy? Did you have great confidence in yourself as a writer?

le Carré: I have a great debt of gratitude to the press for this. In those days English newspapers were much too big to read on the train, so instead of fighting with my colleagues for the *Times*, I would write in little notebooks. I lived a long way out of London. The line has since been electrified, which is a great loss to literature. In those days it was an hour and a half each way. To give the best of the day to your work is most important. So if I could write for an hour and a half on the train, I was already completely jaded by the time I got to the office to start work. And then there was a resurgence of talent during the lunch hour. In the evening something again came back to me. I was always very careful to give my country second-best.

Interviewer: What sorts of things were you writing in these little notebooks?

le Carré: I was writing the very first book, without any kind of skeleton, without any conscious model, but with this odd character, George Smiley, to go along with me. I've never been able to write a book without one very strong character in my rucksack. The moment I had Smiley as a figure, with that past, that memory, that uncomfortable private life and that excellence in his profession, I knew I had something I could live with and work with.

Interviewer: Do you always start with this image of character, rather than, say, plot?

le Carré: Yes, usually somebody. In fact, I can't remember setting off on my travels without some picture of a character to take with me. It really is a companion. I was traveling once in northeast Laos to write a book called *The Honourable Schoolboy*, and I got stuck up with the journalist David Greenway. We had to make a frightful journey to somewhere, and he turned to me and said, "Which class would Smiley travel?" So I said he would definitely be in that one with the wonderful washing urns and all of that—he'd mix with the natives. Greenway says, "I'll tell you what we'll do: we'll put Smiley in there and we'll travel first-class."

Interviewer: You have a wonderful story about the germination of *The Spy Who Came in From the Cold*.

le Carré: That's right. At that time I was very caught up in the Cold War in Germany. I was stationed in Bonn, going to Berlin a lot, and that was the crucible of all that spy commerce in those days. One of my jobs at the embassy, one of my day jobs, you might say, was bringing over German dignitaries, introducing them to British politicians, and functioning as interpreter. I was sitting alone in London Airport, minding my own business, when a very rough-edged, kind of Trevor Howard figure, walked in and sat himself at the bar beside me. He fished in his pocket, put down a great handful of change in heaven-knows-which currencies and denominations, and then said, "A large scotch." Between him and the barman, they just sorted out the money. He drank the scotch and left. I thought I picked up a very slight Irish accent. And that was really all, but there was a deadness in the face, and he looked, as we would have said in the spy world in those days, as if he'd had the hell posted out of him. It was the embodiment, suddenly, of somebody that I'd been looking for. It was he, and I never spoke to him, but he was my guy, Alec Leamas, and I knew he was going to die at the Berlin Wall.

Interviewer: What happens then? You have your character; what process follows?

le Carré: The process is empathy, fear and dramatization. I have to put him into conflict with something, and that conflict usually comes from within. They're usually people who are torn in some way between personal and institutional loyalty. Then there's external conflict. "The cat sat on the mat" is not the beginning of a story, but "The cat sat on the dog's mat" *is*. I take him with me, and I know his habits and manners. I take my tailor to Panama, not knowing anything about the place, and immediately plunge myself into the rag trade, the clothing business. Speaking for my man, Harry Pendel, I inquire all over the place. What would be the chances of setting up a bespoke tailoring business to make really smart suits? I went so far as to visit estate agents and look at potential shops. I talked to the big wholesalers, who said, "Yes, possibly, for bespoke tailoring, if you could invent the taste in Panama, and you could really win people away from buying Armani suits, then it would work. If it became the fashion, if it became the rage, if suddenly in the Union Club in Panama it was impossible to be seen without a Pendel & Braithwaite suit, it would work." So without actually buying the place and buying the stock, I get as realistic an appraisal of the possibilities of his life as I can. I go and find a house for him. I decided to marry him to a Zonian, who's a kind of hybrid of American and Panamanian, a woman who'd been brought up in the Canal Zone, but who was American by sentiment and culture and birth. I took the trouble to mix with people with that kind of background. But I was very much doing Harry's job for him, and I don't think that writers have much center, really. I feel much more like an actor looking for a part. I put on Pendel's clothes in my own mind. Similarly, if I'm some other character, if I'm in the previous book, which was also partly set in Panama, if I'm an old Brit spy waiting for his Joe, his agent, to turn up at the Continental Hotel in Panama, then I'll spend a few hours doing his job, watching the people go by, trying internally to evoke the tension of that moment. "Is it he, is it he? Who is it? Can't see . . ." and so on.

Interviewer: Does your wife worry about these communion-like experiences?
le Carré: She's pretty used to it. It's better than being married to one person.

Interviewer: Does anybody help you with the research? Do you have an assistant?
le Carré: I try, as in the spy trade, to find a really good local contact. Sometimes it's a journalist; in this case, it was an American novelist of distinction called Richard Koster, who lives in Panama. Dick and I became buddies. He marked my card a good deal, said, "These are the people to talk to." And then after that you start leapfrogging. I meet *you* through Dick, and you say, "Well, the chap you should really talk to is so-and-so." Six people down the line you find yourself sitting with an arms dealer in a nightclub, and somebody's really talking about himself. The thing is, if you are a good listener and not adversarial, people love to talk about themselves.

Interviewer: Do you make tape recordings?
le Carré: No, I have a notebook, but all the notes I take are subjective, so that even the notes will be about the characters. Good lines will be given to the characters; they don't just exist as plain lines. So there's some kind of constant interaction between the fantasy that I brought with me to the location—the place as character—and what happens to me after that, the way the fantasy takes on some semblance of truth. What we want is not authenticity; it is credibility. In order to be credible, you have to dress the thing in clothes of authenticity.

Interviewer: How much control do you have over the characters? Does the book ever take completely unexpected turns?

le Carré: All the turns are unexpected because I never impose much on the plot. Once I had Pendel and his Zonian wife and the baddie coming into the shop, I was as nervous and excited about what would happen as I hope the reader is. I don't have charts and so forth. Like a moviemaker, I have a vision of what the audience will see as they leave the theatre, what will be the last image in their heads. In this case, it's the conflagration of Panama. I knew when I started playing with the satire of Panama and that wayward, extraordinary war that the United States fought there—ultimately for good reasons, but initially for very bad ones—that I wanted that to be repeated. I wanted a cycle of history to occur. When you're my age, you have the feeling sometimes that you're seeing the show come round again. For all the flailing and huffing and puffing, there is a kind of fatality about the process of war-making and the excuses we find for it, the consolation of belligerence in politics.

Interviewer: There's a very different tone in *The Tailor of Panama*, isn't there?
le Carré: It's much bouncier. I've got more than one string to my bow, and I thought I'd give this one a twang. If you see the world as gloomily as I see it, the only thing to do is laugh or shoot yourself. My guy does both.

Interviewer: It has been said the book mirrors what you feel about England at the moment.
le Carré: While abroad, I don't want to talk gloomily about my country. I've become interested recently not in the macro-interpretation of my country, but the micro-interpretation. I live in a tiny, desolate part of England, where the real effects of what I see as terrible misgovernment—central misgovernment—can be felt in detail upon agriculture, fishing, communication and transport, all of those things. My definition of a decent society is one that first of all takes care of its losers, and protects its weak. What I see in my country, progressively over these years, is that the rich have got richer, the poor have got poorer. The rich have become indifferent through a philosophy of greed, and the poorer have become hopeless because they're not properly cared for. That's actually something that is happening in many western societies. Your own, I am told, is not free from it. It's certainly something one could see in process in the microcosm of Panama. There are vastly rich people there. Insiders will tell you that the country is still run by about thirty people, people who generate huge wealth and carve the thing up between themselves. Yet it's a brand-new country from lunchtime on the thirty-first of December, 1999.

It will have total independence, having been a colony under the Colombians, the French and the Americans. The canal will revert to their own possession. And we have the fascinating sight of a small country identifying itself, finding out who it will be. All sorts of people are waiting for a slice of the cake. Despite appalling unemployment and an appalling poverty record, they have it within their grasp to even out their society. But by what method is anyone's guess. I tried to play one perception of the country against my own domestic concerns.

Interviewer: Did you have this attitude before you began your research in Panama?
le Carré: It was something that dawned on me years earlier, actually. I went to Panama seven or eight years ago just to write one passage for *The Night Manager*. There was a drug dealer in that book who was buying arms, and there was a British arms dealer who was selling him the arms. When I was in Miami I asked the drug-enforcement people and the arms-control people where one would go to negotiate these transactions, and they said with one voice, "Panama. Go to the Free Zone of Colon. You can buy and sell anything you want." I said, "What about a firepower demonstration?" and they said, "That's fine, just go up to the Costa Rican border. Everybody does it there."

Interviewer: What does that mean—tanks and F-16s?
le Carré: Whatever you wanted. You can buy a little quiet, everyone will be cleared out of the area, and then you can do what you want. After meeting a number of arms dealers and people like that, I had a sense of the very venal nature of Panama. I think they're trying to work on it, to get their act together for independence. What I saw was a Casablanca without heroes, and I thought I had to come back. But then I experienced the delight of recognizing that it—the country, I mean—was writing its own ticket for the year 2000. And the whole farce of the last American colony being handed over—we colonial Brits know what that means. The comedy built into that is irresistible.

Interviewer: So you did not have trouble finding adversarial situations for your heroes after the cold war.
le Carré: No, I really loved it. I'm not saying that I made the transition easily. I think I stumbled a couple of times. All sorts of things that I'd got too used to were taken away. But I never wanted to write about Smiley again. I felt it was done, and I don't like writing through an old man's eyes. You know, the

older you get, the younger you want to be. Also, I didn't want to go back to that morbid face-off—I mean my stories were getting frozen into the ice. All of a sudden everything was up for grabs. It was extremely comic that the uninformed were saying that spying is over, hence le Carré is over. The one thing you can bet is that spying is never over. Spying is like the wiring in this building: it's just a question of who takes it over and switches on the lights. It will go on and on and on.

Interviewer: But is espionage not different since the end of the cold war? Do you still keep in touch with spies?

le Carré: I have a few people, Americans mainly, some Israelis. The Brits don't talk to me. It's necessary to understand what real intelligence work is. It will never cease. It's absolutely essential that we have it. At its best, it is simply the left arm of healthy governmental curiosity. It brings to a strong government what it needs to know. It's the collection of information, a journalistic job, if you will, but done in secret. All the rest of it—intervention, destabilization, assassination, all that junk—is in my view not only anticonstitutional but unproductive and silly. You can never foresee the consequences. But it's a good job as long as intelligence services collect sensible information and report it to their governments, and as long as that intelligence is properly used, thought about and evaluated. Then you come to the question of targets of intelligence: what are the proper targets of the CIA? That's a policy problem. For me, they are much more widespread than you would suppose. I think they should be extended to the ecology, to the pollution of rivers and those things. There is, for example, one plant in northern Russia that disseminates more pollution than the whole of Scandinavia. One plant alone. I think things of that sort are so life-threatening that they should be included in the CIA's brief. And counter-terrorism: you cannot make a case for not spying on terrorist organizations. You've got to spy the hell out of them. But countersubversion—that's a really murky target. That is when a government defines what political thoughts are poisonous to the nation, and I find that a terribly dangerous area. And then of course the maverick weapons—they've been left all over the place, partly by us. I mean, where are the Stingers we gave to the Afghans? Also, if you meddle in people's affairs, you then have to live with the consequences. Look at Afghan-istan. We recruited the Muslim extremist movement to assist us in the fight against Russia and we let loose a demon. Intervention is a very dangerous game, and it always has consequences, and they are almost always embarrassing.

Interviewer: Which is the best of the secret services?

le Carré: You know, it's a bit like schoolmastering: you can never quite tell how good the next chap is. You never see your colleagues at work. If you get one good source—while the CIA and the British had Penkovsky, for example, they had acres of absolutely wonderful material, and they were putting it out under different source-names, for reasons of security—then you look absolutely great to your paymasters. But when Penkovsky ended, suddenly they were all dressed up and had nowhere to go. They looked awful. I am sure that the best intelligence services must still be Israel's. They've made awful mistakes, as intelligence services will, but that's because Mossad and Shin Bet are splendidly motivated. If Israel loses a battle, it loses the war; if it loses the war, it loses its country. Everybody in Israel knows what security means, and everybody pulls together. There is no political division between the parties on the subject of security, not until you get to the anguished problems of settlements and so forth. So they are not only the best, and have a very long tradition of being so, but they're the best-motivated. It's much harder now to evaluate the Brits or the Americans or anyone else. As I say, I know next to nothing about the Brits, but what I do hear is that they're far better than they used to be.

Interviewer: Did you know Philby?

le Carré: No, I didn't. Philby was my secret sharer whom I never met. By the time I went into the secret world, as I now know, Philby had passed my name to his Russian controllers. It's a very curious feeling to know that every halfway-perilous thing one did was already known to the Russians miles ahead. I mean I know that good men are scarce. I did not do anything very dangerous or brave. The older you get, the braver you get. I wasn't very brave. And no, I didn't know Philby. When I went to Moscow for the first time, in 1987, I met a man called Gendrik Borovik who said, "There's a very good friend of mine, excellent patriot from your country who would like to meet with you. His name is Kim Philby." I said, "Gendrik, you can't possibly do that to me. I'm going to the ambassador's for dinner tomorrow night. I can't be the guest of the Queen's ambassador one night, and the Queen's biggest traitor the next. It won't do."

Interviewer: I'm surprised you could resist it.

le Carré: I know, it was tough to resist but I did. The invitation was renewed and I still wouldn't go. Then a British journalist, Phil Knightly, went and saw

Philby right at the end of his life. Philby knew he was dying. Knightly said, "What do you think of le Carré?" Philby replied, "I don't know. I quite like the books, but the fellow doesn't care for me. He must know something about me." So I puzzled about that. And I think in fact I did know something about him. Kim Philby had a monstrous father, St. John Philby, who ended up selling Rolls-Royces to King Fahd in Saudi Arabia and acting as his advisor. He became a Muslim convert and had a couple of wives—two or three. In fact, I think Fahd gave him a wife. He became a very powerful, unpleasant and anti-British figure in our peculiar empire. Kim grew up under this tyrannous old monster, and when Kim was twelve or thirteen, his father gave him to the Bedouin to be turned into a man. Kim went off into the desert. This was a boy who then went to English public school. I think that the cumulative effect of having such a ferocious father, and a mother he barely knew, produced in him some kind of natural dissenting nature. Indeed he became a subvert. I think he really carried, metaphorically, a pistol in his pocket for the whole of society. If anything embraced him, he wanted to kill it.

I went through a comparable, though perhaps less vicious version of that with my own peculiar papa, who was in and out of prison. He was tremendously dominating. I too had no mother through these years. I felt, thinking about Philby and his father, and myself and my father, that there could have been a time when I, if properly spoken to by the right wise man or woman, could have been seduced into some kind of underground act of revenge against society.

Interviewer: Now that you no longer write on the train to London, what is your working day like?

le Carré: Well, I still don't type. I write by hand, and my wife types everything up, endlessly, repeatedly. I correct by hand too. I am an absolute monk about my work. It's like being an athlete: you have to find out which are the best hours of the day. I'm a morning person. I like to drink in the evening, go to sleep on a good idea and wake up with the idea solved or advanced. I believe in sleep. And I go straight to work, often very early. If a book's getting to the end of its run, I'll start at four-thirty or five o'clock in the morning and go through to lunchtime. In the afternoon I'll take a walk, and then, over a scotch, take a look at what Jane's typed out, and fiddle with it a bit more. But I always try to go to sleep before I finish working, just a little bit before. Then I know where I'll go the next morning, but I won't quite know what I am going to do when I go. And then in the morning it seems to deliver the answer.

For the last few years I have lived only in the deep country. I've always kept away from writers and the literary set. I'd much rather talk to the woodcutter than a fellow writer. I like the primary material. I don't like exchanging ideas much. I don't like talking about my work, believe it or not. I'm a total bore, actually.

Interviewer: With this monkish routine, how many words do you produce each day?
le Carré: I don't know. When it's going well it goes terribly fast. It isn't at all surprising to write a chapter in a day, which for me is about twenty-two pages. When it's going badly, it isn't really going badly; it's just the beginning. The first page and the first chapter are a matter of endless fiddling, cutting out all the good bits, putting in a whole lot of verbiage. Actually, it's my only way of thinking. Without a pen in my hand I can't think. And by the way, not every aspect of the monk is observed.

Interviewer: What are the "good" parts you cut out? Do you keep them for further use?
le Carré: The good parts are usually the bits of gorgeous prose that stick out like sore thumbs. No, I have never made use of them later. If I fish them out of a drawer, they usually embarrass me and I chuck them away.

Interviewer: Do you go from *A* to *Z* or do you bounce all over the place?
le Carré: I go from *A* to *Z*, but via a whole lot of hieroglyphics we've never met.

Interviewer: What do you say to Norman Rush, who charged you with anti-Semitism in his review of *The Tailor of Panama*?[3]

3. "Spying and Lying," *The New York Times Book Review* (20 October 1996), 11: "But a more substantial defect for me lies in an aspect of the Pendel character: here we have, however little Mr. le Carré intended it, yet another literary avatar of Judas. It's reasonable to make an expatriate British tailor a Jew, but does this Jew, for example, have to defame the only decent, 'saintly' (Pendel's own term) political leader in Panama, and then go on to implicate his own wife's utterly innocent Christian study group to boot?" le Carré and Rush exchanged letters in *The New York Times Book Review* on November 3 and 17, 1996. le Carré refuted Rush's charge in "Nervous Times," a 1998 address to the Anglo-Israel Society; le Carré's denial that his novel was anti-Semitic triggered an exchange of angry letters with Salman Rushdie in the London *Guardian*.

le Carré: I tell you, I have had some pretty big tomatoes thrown at me in my time, but this one missed. This one is completely nutty. For those of you who don't know—and I imagine the whole of New York knows—I am a red-toothed anti-Semite. And the reason for this, according to today's *Times*, is that my beloved Harry Pendel, who is the very heart of the story, is described by the writer of this piece as a Jew. Now, you and I know perfectly well that in Jewish law a Jew has to have a Jewish mum. Harry Pendel's mum was an Irish Catholic. That's our first problem. However, I made Pendel a mixture of different traditions, as I myself am a mixture of different traditions—son of a criminal, working-class kid, sent to a smart school, learned to speak proper. He was my cocktail. He was the equivalent of me in literary terms. I am told by today's Sunday *Times* that he is a Judas Iscariot avatar. Now Hindus in the audience may be distressed by this misuse of *avatar*, and I hope that political correctness will assert itself, and that the gentleman will apologize to Hindus for misusing these religious symbols. I can only say that it simply isn't me; he's writing about a mirage, he's writing about something in his own head. All my life, ever since I started writing, because of the extraordinary childhood I had—the early introduction to the refugee problem in central Europe and what not—I have been fascinated, enchanted, drawn to and horrified by the plight of middle-European Jews. It has infected my writing—book number one, book number three, *The Spy Who Came in From the Cold*, I could go on. It is the one issue in my own life on which I may say I have a clean record. I just want to say that. And if I blame anyone, it is only the *New York Times*. All writers write dotty stuff; I do the same. The editor should have said, "This guy's gone off the reservation." If there's anybody here connected with that paper, I hope they'll go back and, I don't know, light a fire or something.

Interviewer: In every book of yours there seems to be a division between the first hundred pages and the rest of the story, which tends to be much clearer than the initial section. Why is that?

le Carré: I have bad habits, like we all do, and one of them is to spend much too much time on the first hundred pages of a book. I always think that if I had another life, I would write the first hundred pages and then start again. It's a principle of mine to come into the story as late as possible, and to tell it as fast as you can. The later you join the story, the more quickly you draw the audience into the middle. But beginning late requires a lot of retrospective stuff, and that's a problem I think I will always be dealing with.

Interviewer: Your characters always seem to be searching for their own identities.

le Carré: Yes, that's true, but it's part of the golden center that one can never touch. I'm looking for mine, they're looking for theirs.

Interviewer: Do you set out intending to say something about morality?

le Carré: No, it isn't as altruistic as that. I think it's the unconscious, irreconcilable fact inside one's own self, feeling a very flawed person and really making a search through the possibilities of one's own character. I think that most of my books are part of some process of self-education, often about the places I go to. Most of all, they are about the peculiar tension between institutional loyalty and loyalty to oneself; the mystery of patriotism, for a Brit of my age and generation, where it runs, how it should be defined, what it's worth and what a corrupting force it can be when misapplied. All that stuff is just in me and it comes out in the characters. I don't mean to preach, but I know I do, and I'm a very flawed person. It's quite ridiculous.

Interviewer: A number of books purporting to be guides to your work have been published. What do you think of these and do you cooperate with the authors?

le Carré: I haven't read any of them. I became very embarrassed by that stuff. But of course I was very proud, as anybody would be, of creating a private world out of the real one, and of making it work in literary terms. After three BBC television series of my stuff, I began to get withdrawal symptoms about the Smiley cult and the le Carré cult. I didn't want to be that person. One way of dealing with that was simply to refuse to read the critical spin-off, and refuse to take notice of it. *The Tailor of Panama* is the first book in a long time on which I have read reviews. Usually Jane reads them. I always argue that you should not accept the value of good reviews, because if you do you have to accept the bad ones.

Interviewer: What is it like to talk to an arms dealer?

le Carré: I just do my absolute best to be a fly on the wall. The most acute moment of this sort was when I went to Moscow to explore for *Our Game*. I went with the Chechen and the Ingush groups that were hanging around in Moscow. All I wanted to do, exactly as when I was with the Palestinians in south Lebanon, was listen, find out what made them tick, just listen. But I also wanted to meet a Russian mafia boss, and through a variety of contacts, mainly ex-KGB people, it was finally made possible for me at two or three in the morning to meet Dima. Dima came into the nightclub, which he owned and which was guarded by young men with Kalashnikovs and grenades strapped to their belts. He came in wearing Ray-Bans with his hookers and his men and his people. He looked like the Michelin Man, he was so blown up with steroids. The music was so loud I had to kneel down to get close enough to his ear to talk to him, so I seemed to be actually kneeling in his presence. My interpreter was kneeling beside me. Dima gave me the whole spiel about how "Russia is anarchic. . . . yes, I've killed people; yes, I've done this and that . . . but actually I've done nothing against the law; it was all self-defense. Anyway, the law doesn't work for post-communist Russia." And I said, "Dima, let me ask you a question. In the United States, great crooks have with time become serious members of society. They've built museums and hospitals and stadiums. When, Dima, do you think that you might feel it was necessary to take on your responsibility for your grandchildren, your great grandchildren?" Dima started talking and my interpreter all of a sudden fell into a dark silence. I said, "What is it, Vladimir? What's he saying?" He said, "Mr. David, I am very sorry, but he says fuck off."

Interviewer: Have you ever considered writing more nonfiction, to add to the scattering of articles you have already written?
le Carré: I think that for as long as I can do the novel, and I really feel the buzz, that's what I should do. Also, the professional deformation of persistent fiction writing makes it very hard to stick to the truth. It's an awful thing to say, but I've almost ceased to be an accurate reporter, because the systems and the cogs won't stop turning. I have to get it down very quickly and stick to it, or I start embroidering in no time.

Interviewer: How do you settle on an ending?
le Carré: Most of the endings are apocalyptic. I don't believe I've ever doubted endings. I play around endlessly with the beginning and the middle, but the end is always a goal. Certainly, when I saw the Berlin Wall going up—I was there to flesh out our station in Berlin—when I conceived that story *The Spy Who Came in From the Cold* which I wrote in five weeks, I was determined that he would be killed at the wall. They both would. *A Perfect Spy* and *The Tailor of Panama* had to be ended with a forfeit. It's the Gothic gloom that takes over in me at some point.

Interviewer: Did you ever want to be an actor or write for the stage?
le Carré: I've often thought of writing for the stage. Other people always think that I should be an actor, and once, catastrophically, I appeared in one of my own films. I had about eight words to say, and we did sixteen takes. George Roy Hill[4] kept looking at me and saying, "David, that's too broad. David, that's dull. Do it again." Either he was just torturing me or I was as bad as I think I was.

Novel writing spoils you, that's the problem. In novel writing, you dress the stage, you dress your characters, you know exactly how they speak, you know in your own imagination exactly how they look. You want everybody to have a different perception of them. I think I'm forfeit for the stage, as I am for screenwriting. I simply cannot entrust the other jobs to other people. It's a strange thing, but it's so.

Interviewer: How did you develop the character of Jim Prideaux in *Tinker, Tailor, Soldier, Spy*?
le Carré: Jim Prideaux was a schoolmaster who had been terribly betrayed by a man he greatly loved in the British secret services. I taught quite a lot when I was young. Before I taught at Eton I taught at a school for disadvantaged kids. During that time I met a lot of the strange underlife of Brits who go into private-school teaching. There was a very good schoolmaster at one of the schools where I taught—a big, rugged fellow with a limp. I used to think that that was the outer shell for Jim. And in that story Jim was set against a little boy who was a watcher, a little spy fellow. In fact, that child was written into my life because I was a duty master one night at this school for disadvantaged kids, and somebody came to me and said, "Please, Jameson is trying to kill himself." They took me to this stairwell in a big Victorian house, and there was a little kid standing on the banister at the top, with a marble floor forty feet below. Everyone was petrified. And I just went and scooped him up. He didn't jump. And when we were alone I said, "Why did you do that?" He said, "I just can't do the routine. I can't make my bed. I can never make it to class promptly. Everybody teases me." It was that little child in *Tinker, Tailor, Soldier, Spy* whom Jim Prideaux espoused: they make a common bond. I love people who can spot a victim, and Jim could because he was one himself.

4. Director of *The Little Drummer Girl* (1984).

Interviewer: What is your opinion of ex-Stasi chief Markus Wolf? Did he help inspire you to create Karla?

le Carré: Markus Wolf was the head boy of East German intelligence, the branch that was charged with spying on West Germany. He was imprisoned briefly after the wall came down and Germany was unified. He was brought before a constitutional court in Karlsruhe, I think—they tried to put him inside for all the bad stuff he'd done. And one of the things that was said about Markus Wolf was that he had been the model for my character Fiedler in *The Spy Who Came in From the Cold*. Now, that is, in a word, sheer nonsense. I knew nothing of Markus Wolf when I wrote *The Spy Who Came in From the Cold*. If you want my personal opinion, it's a brand of postwar euphoria that I absolutely loathe. "Actually, your Spitfires were nearly as good as our Messerchmitts." In my view, Markus Wolf knowingly served a completely corrupt and disgusting regime, and there was no justification whatever for the methods he used. I think that Markus Wolf is the modern equivalent of Albert Speer. I think that sooner or later, instead of being a good German, he will be revealed for the nasty little twerp he was.

Interviewer: One last question. If you could construct a composite writer, what attributes would be conferred?

le Carré: I would give a composite writer all the virtues I have not got, but the trouble is, I am not sure he would be able to write. I would give him clarity of vision, independence of public acclaim, the early experience of happy heterosexual love between two good parents and a voracious appetite for other people's writing. Then I would fall asleep.

Secrets and Lies

Alan Franks / 1999

Reprinted from *The Times* [London], 13 February 1999, pp. 18–23.
Copyright © *The Times*. Reprinted by permission.

The cold hung on long after the break-up of the Soviet Union. It deepened with the decade, and reports suggested it was hardening into a permafrost. It was impossible to gauge the truth since the man himself was not talking. He was more remote than ever, shunning London and only breaking his silences for short, splenetic bursts. It was impossible to get to him through his friends, even if you knew who they were, as they were all so discreet, or dead, or oversees. And so he took on the air of Eighties Edward Heath,[1] digging in for the long winter of the new order.

The photograph was interesting. It made him implacably handsome in the set English manner. A face fashioned for top surveillance and outdoor pursuits. The same image kept on being used in publicity material and newspaper articles, as tends to happen when a famous person has stopped playing ball with the photographers. This froze him further still into the high landscape of cold shoulders, while his own face got on with its life and turned into something completely different.

John le Carré's silence has gone on, in England at least, for years. If you insist that this can only be explained by a conspiracy theory, then you have read too much of the wrong stuff and will be brought up short. And if you are in my game, you will be brought up very short indeed. Nothing to do with conspiracy, he says, but corruption.

Corruption?

"Yes," he says. "I have been approached by this or that literary editor or critic to take a position on a book. They have said we would love you to review this, and then, in brackets, we will look kindly on your own next book. This was some while back. Perhaps it's changed."

He recalls writing "offhand things" in a review of C. P. Snow's *Last Things*, and then being called in by the literary editor to be told that he really

---

1. British Prime Minister (1970–1974); a Conservative, he disagreed with the foreign policy of his Conservative successor Margaret Thatcher.

shouldn't make such remarks. "It was a deal, and the deal was on offer all the time."

And then, a little later: "It has been the fate of the arts since the beginning of time to be spoken about mainly by articulate failures." All this occurs within a few minutes of our meeting, soon enough to reinforce the idea that he prizes forthrightness above diplomacy. The exchanges come after a discussion about his relationship with the critical establishment. A very brief discussion this turned out to be: "It doesn't exist."

Cynics will say that he is only talking now because he has a new novel out, *Single & Single*, and someone somewhere is leaning on him to help shift some product. To be cynical is not necessarily to be wrong. When I ask him why he is suddenly singing, he maintains the candour. "I think I care less. I think I have made my point. I suppose I just want to say I'm around. But people always want to know where I stand on English writing, and I'm just not part of the critical process."

So he bypasses the arbiters who, for the past thirty-five years, have raised his hackles and lowered his critical esteem with the use of the dastardly words "genre writer." He appeals directly to his public, in the certainty that the appeal is enormous. He has seventeen novels to his name, many of them international best-sellers and hits on cinema and television. He is about as wealthy as a British writer can be, and as driven as any man of half his sixty-seven years. He says it is quite good enough for him that a novel as complex as *Tinker, Tailor, Soldier, Spy* should have remained at the top of the US lists for as long as it did. He happily talks to the Germans and the Americans, and lives almost as far from the centre of things as the English map permits. He nurses a complex patriotism which excoriates disloyalty, hates Thatcherism, embraces Europe and would like to state-integrate the public-school system that educated him—or nearly did—and his four grown-up sons.

I ask him if the end of the Cold War ever looked like destroying his fiction's context and environment. That was the fate which was predicted for him in the years after *The Russia House* in 1989, rather as it was predicted that the intelligence and military industries of the West would have to seek out fresh backdrops.

"Ridiculous, says le Carré. "On the day that politicians stop lying, on the day that nations don't produce terror organisations, then maybe . . . no, nothing has changed, except that the supposed stand-off between the two great monoliths has ended. From my point of view that was a great relief.

By the end it was not the aftermath of the Cold War that I was struggling with, but the Cold War itself. I had written four or five books that had nothing to do with it, so I didn't feel that I was attached. We are back to where we were when Eric Ambler was writing, where you select your area, look for the context and tell your story. Yes, there was a period when people decided to write me off because of the end of the Cold War. It was a sort of critical joke, that I had been cut off from my lifeline, and it was sheer nonsense."

We are at his large, underused house in Hampstead. The street is a magnificent oval set around a private garden and so secluded that you could use the flanking streets of the hill for years without being aware of its existence. It once managed to escape the attentions of a London street map and went unrecorded, like a secret installation. His second wife, Jane, whom he married in 1972, has gone on to the heath for a recce with the photographer, or smudger as they call him. I was to have gone down to Cornwall, but the house, just up the coast from Land's End, was having work done it.

A professional associate of the author's told me that I should not be apprehensive about meeting him (le Carré), but that he didn't much like people writing about the inside of his homes. I was asked to send copies of a few previous articles that I had written on eminent authors or other relevant subjects. I was also asked to supply a typed sheet of my own biographical details, rather as if was me who was going to be interviewed. The cuttings request is quite rare, if only because so many famous people are far too interested in themselves to have any time for other lives. As for the potted biog, I had never had such a request, and for similar reasons. It smacked of paranoia—I mean his rather than mine—but it turned out to be nothing of the sort. In fact, as I write this I am aware that I had an utterly misleading picture of him and that I have probably been perpetuating it here. Still, le Carré without a spot of mistaken identity would be a little like Ruth Rendell without a murder. I don't think I have met anyone with such a disparity between the public image and the actuality. Whether he meant to or not, he has probably connived in this through his silence.

The man sitting across the drawing room from me is a world away from the Lone Yachtsman figure in the press bumph. He is soft-spoken, courteous and self-mocking, with the faintly pastoral manner of a liberal housemaster. It is not generally known of him that he took a first-class degree in modern languages from Oxford, and that he taught at Eton as a young man between his periods of intelligence work. He speaks with measured hostility about what he regards as the glorification of defectors from the secret service, and of the "ill-advised" nature of Britain's involvement in the bombing of Iraq.[2] He confesses to being "stiff with inconsistences" and shrugs in resigned amusement. To hear him speak now, late in his strange life of subterfuge and invention, is rather like seeing several men of different persuasions meet at an agreed point to make an accommodation. He talks of the dangers in the newly configured world, of the need for diligent surveillance of Blake[3] and Philby, of his idol Graham Greene—"politically a child"—and of his own strange passage through boyhood. As he describes it, some of the later inconsistences fall into place, just as they do in a good le Carré plot. It was Greene, he remembers, who observed that childhood was a novelist's credit balance, and then he proceeds to demonstrate it. His mother vanished when he was five, and his father was in and out of jail, generally for fraud. So the young David Cornwell, the author's real name, grew up with his brother between the terror of the next knock on the door and the tawdry glamour of the underworld.

He remembers teenage visits to the Albany Club in Old Burlington Street, with the bar and the black-market restaurants on one floor, the illegal betting on the next one, with all the major bookmakers represented, and the girls on the top floor. "They were all there," he says. "The police and the show business people always love the criminals. The Crazy Gang came. My father played snooker with Flanagan and Allen.[4] He gave huge parties out in the suburbs, and the Australian Test cricketers came. I met the Don (Bradman) and Keith Miller.[5] With those credentials he could ask just about anyone into his life, and it was only gradually that people realised they were being conned. He never made any money really."

How, I wonder, were the school fees paid?

"In dried fruit mainly, from the black market. At prep school at any rate. My first stepmother was a wise woman, and I think she made him pay the Sherborne fees. He cared about the education more than anything. He was like Magwitch with Pip in *Great Expectations*. When he was caught in some

2. In December 1998 President Bill Clinton ordered the bombing of Iraq because Saddam Hussein had failed to cooperate with U.N. weapons inspectors.

3. George Blake, Dutch-born British citizen, who was exposed in 1961 as a Soviet spy.

4. Bud Flanagan and Chesney Allen were the principal members of The Crazy Gang, a British comedy group.

5. Bradman and Miller were prominent Australian cricket players.

heinous situation, or a bit of truth came out, he would say, 'Everything I've ever done has been for you. You can do anything you want in life; you can be a barrister or a solicitor.' He was always fond of defending himself in court, although he generally did so without success."

This father, Ronnie, comes over like some lovable bounder from the pages of Joyce Cary or Patrick Hamilton.[6] In a memorable scene from his life, which trumps fiction, he stood for Parliament as a Liberal candidate. It was a means of bunking off military duties on the grounds of national importance. "I helped him in Yarmouth in 1950," le Carré recalls. "Most of his helpers had done time with him. One night I got back from loudspeaker canvassing to the Commercial Hotel, which we had taken over as HQ, and everyone's looking very solemn. My Dad goes, 'Son, we've got to talk,' with this very sanctimonious voice. He says he's had this strange conversation with the agent of the Conservative Party. 'He's said that if I continue with the campaign, they're going to let it be known that many years ago I had certain difficulties, and I went to prison, being in the position of the office boy who had taken a few stamps out of the box and was caught before he had a chance to put them back. The question is, do we fight or do we give in?'

"I say, 'We fight,' and they all go, 'Told you he had it in him, Ronnie.' Three nights later we go in the Bentley, driven by Mr Nutbeam. Ronnie's half-pissed, although he passes himself off as someone who's taken the pledge. He does the speech and he says, 'I want to leave you with this thought. People come up to me in the street and they say, "Why are you fighting this campaign? You must be very idealistic." And I reply, "Ideals are rather like the stars. We cannot reach them but we profit by their presence." ' Then a woman says, 'Is it true the candidate was in prison?' And Ronnie says, 'I see here mothers and fathers and people of a certain age whose children and grandchildren have gone out into the world, and I want to ask: which one of you, when that child has made a mistake and paid the price . . . would slam the door in his face?' " Tumultuous cheering, applause, weeping, and embracing. In his next address the same question was asked from the floor, the same answer was given and with the same reaction. Encouraged by the success of the previous occasion, Ronnie had planted a questioner in the audience. He was, says le Carré, a complete fantasist, genuinely charming, "but the bodies on the trail were

6. Cary (1888–1957) created the roguish artist Gulley Jimson in *The Horse's Mouth* (1944); Hamilton (1904–1962) wrote murder/suspense novels that often featured colorful characters and locales.

pretty awful." At home in Chalfont St. Peter they would park the cars in the back garden, put out all the lights in one side of the house and sit in the other. If a neighbour called, the likelihood was that money was owed. And if one opened the door, there was the problem over what to say of Ronnie's whereabouts.

"Adulthood was a dangerous place. From an early age I felt I was living on occupied territory. Because of the life we lived, I have mistrusted anything that looked respectable. I always believed it was a sham. I saw Ronnie in majestic clothes, speaking well, with the regional accent somehow laundered out of him, and lying through his teeth. Still now my hackles go up secretly when meeting leading politicians. I've never believed that what I saw was true. You come into the house and I'm thinking, is he really from *The Times*? It's always that tiny paranoid blip as I open the door: what should I be thinking?" A little like Smiley.

"Yes, like Smiley. For him the most dangerous place is home."

Perhaps the wariness has served him well in the past.

"The inside-out thinking becomes a habit of mind very fast. You are always looking at the reverse side of the coin, the other possibilities: why is he here? Who sent him? What can the agenda be?" If Graham Greene's recurrent themes of friendship and betrayal owed everything to his dealings with Carter and Wheeler as schoolboys in Berkhamsted,[7] so it seems that le Carré's sense of duplicity in the fabric of authority is a legacy from Ronnie. As is his savouring of honour among misfits and marginals and his perception of dishonourable schoolboys in the heart of the establishment.

His own story is as complex as his characters. At sixteen he decides to leave Sherborne. Ronnie insists the boy tell the school himself and so le Carré faces an outraged and unforgiving housemaster. Then he goes to university in Bern, with £100 and "a memory of England that was like hell." He embraces German culture and identity with the passion of the unanchored. "I wanted to grow a second soul, to have a fresh identity as a substitute for the English experience."

But then the National Service, and intelligence work on account of the German. Then Oxford, and the stint teaching at Eton. Always this compulsion to go back to the sources of his ambivalence about the country and the people who run it. "Yes, that's the paradox, isn't it. It's the same with Smiley. He

---

7. Lionel A. Carter and A. H. Wheeler were schoolmates of Greene who tormented him.

loved the institution and constantly saw the flaws. The establishment he didn't love, although he moved in it and married in it. I was drawn to Eton by a great sense of service, which paradoxically I still feel. Look, if I could resolve it, I probably wouldn't write."

From 1960 to 1964 he worked for the Foreign Service. He has, in the past, played the self-effacement card over this and made noises about a desk job in Bonn. But there was clearly more to it. It has been suggested he was already passing on information about his left-inclined university contemporaries.

"I can't take a proper position on that because I can't describe the context. But even if that were the case, if that's all I did, I don't know that it's such a disgraceful thing to have done, if you look at the record of people who were recruited at university from the ranks of Communist sympathisers and later turned into traitors to their country." I ask if he was ever drawn into deceitful behavior that was to trouble his conscience and he answers no, without hesitation.

"Largely the justification for what we did was one I accepted and still accept. That doesn't mean the work was pleasant. It could often be quite disgusting in the sense that you had to penetrate a settled organisation of people who trusted each other and invite informants to come forward and say whether their employers and employees were Communists, that sort of stuff . . . but somebody has to clean the drains, and I found that I did do things that, although they were in some way morally repugnant, I felt at the time, and still feel, to have been necessary . . . the same people who say it's disgusting that dons should be reporting on undergraduates and their opinions, which happened during the Cold War, ask why we didn't know about Blunt, Philby, Burgess and Maclean.

"I can find nothing whatever sinister in keeping files on big names. The people who find that outrageous are the ones who then complain we didn't know about something else. There is simply no compatibility between the two prejudices."

What a strange country, he suggests, where whistle-blowers such as David Shayler and Richard Tomlinson, former MI5 and MI6 officers respectively, are accorded a more heroic status than the silent and diligent agent.[8] "We wouldn't cross the road to shake hands with an army deserter, but there is a particular vindictiveness about the public attitude (towards the intelligence

8. Members of British intelligence who were dismissed for threatening to reveal agency secrets.

service) that I just don't understand. What's the beef? Is it that it shouldn't exist, or is it that it's no good? For as long as you have an Irish threat, international terrorism and crime, for as long as we are a moving target for all sorts of angry minorities, you have to have an organisation that monitors these people."

One of his own most admired operations is to have made the world of his books so persuasive. It is as if he has kept his access to some impeccable source for the thirty-five years since his relatively brief involvement. He has a number of explanations. First, he maintains that once you have known the nature of the thing, it is really quite easy to imagine the state of our administrative subconscious at a given time. He adds that it is not too hard to obtain information about British services from foreigners. In his new book there is a premise that there is a joint team comprising elements of MI5, Customs, GCHQ, SAS and others, and that they will merge and function operationally without regard to their respective service loyalties.

"The logic of that," he says, "is inescapable in the present climate. Where I could, I checked out the possibility of this, and quickly had it confirmed that this is the way they like to work."

He likes to work as he has for most of his writing life, starting at 6 a.m. and doing the voices out loud. He does a terrific Alec Guinness and sundry characters of elocuted poshness who have surely come from Ronnie. He performs them to his amanuensis wife as she keys his longhand into the computer. If anyone knows where the bodies are buried it is she, but I doubt they come more loyal than this.

He says he was never happier politically than in the wake of the last election. "It was simply amazing, the notion that one was never again going to be lectured by Michael Howard[9] on the virtues of extending prison sentences; that all those faces and voices were going. That Blair had managed to deliver this divided and diverse party made me think he was a tough egg. But I don't know what he is tough about . . . he needs two or three terms. I just don't like him echoing Mrs Thatcher."

Surely le Carré's patriotism made him sympathetic to her defense posture. "On the contrary. In terms of national status that foreign policy was the perpetuation of an illusion; the preference of the 'special relationship' with

9. Howard served as Home Secretary (1993–1997) under Conservative Prime Minister John Major (1990–1997), who was defeated by Labour Party candidate Tony Blair in 1997.

the US over our European link. I thought Blair was an absolute fool to
embark on that raid (on Iraq), and that it was timed for the obvious reasons.
It seems to have achieved nothing except the possible further aggrandisement
of Hussein."

His position might not come as such a surprise to those who read his
previous novel, *The Tailor of Panama*, with its ringing condemnation of the
establishment and its institutions. "It was a strong attack. But then by the end
of Mrs Thatcher, some terrible things had happened to this country. There
was a licensing of greed and the abolition of the mutual caring which should
characterise Britain. During that period, some really bad things happened,
from which we will take an awfully long time to recover: the elevation of the
cultureless oaf as money-earner; the destruction of culture itself because it
was a threat to the aims of pure materialism. These are mystical things, not
easily quantifiable by the historian."

As for the still less visible world of official secrets, I don't think it engages
le Carré as an observable stratum of corporate behaviour nearly so much as
it does as a metaphor for the individual condition. From him there are no
prizes for this conclusion, as he suspected the truth of it before he even
started to write. "As a young man, you expect that there is some great safe
with the nation's secrets in it, and that you will discover, as Goethe said, what
the world holds at its innermost point. Then you find out that it's the same
show as the outside world, with the same petty ambitions, factions and
wars. . . . most of us have tenuous relations with our organisations and
institutions. Take your newspaper. Where do you stand there? What kind of
putsch has there been while you're away?" Someone has slipped the paranoia
into my tea, and it's time to go. He escorts me up the road, with the manners
of a good host in a strange country. We walk to the Tube station in the dusk,
through the land of Melvyn Bragg and Alfred Brendel, Michael Foot and the
shade of Kingsley Amis.[10] The houses are imposing, classical, tasteful, large.
But now that I come to look at them, there is barely a light on in any of them.

10. Bragg (1939–) is a writer and television figure; Brendel (1931–) is a classical pianist; Foot
(1913–) was a Labour M.P.; Amis (1922–1995) was a novelist.

David Cornwell Discusses His Novel *Absolute Friends*, Which Was Written under His Pen Name, John le Carré

Robert Siegel / 2004

Transcription of interview from *All Things Considered*, National Public Radio, February 4, 2004. Copyright © 2004 NPR. Reprinted by permission.

Interviewer: *Absolute Friends* is the title of the latest novel by John le Carré, the pen name of David Cornwell. It is a tale full of those trademark themes of le Carré's spy novels: loyalty, betrayal, and, as the title suggests, friendship. David Cornwell joins us from London.

Welcome to the program, once again.

le Carré: Thank you very much.

Interviewer: More than once in reading your books, I've been reminded of that quotation attributed to E. M. Forster in 1938: "If I had to choose between betraying my country and betraying my friend, I hope that I should have the guts to betray my country." Do you regard this as a very vital tension between friendship and patriotism, a theme that you've been writing about for many years?

le Carré: I think, yes. In this book, I have, I suppose, explored that problem almost as far as it will go. And I think the reason for that is that our perception of nationhood is becoming very important to us, even as a process of internationalization theoretically occurs. And also, we're living in a time when patriotism is invoked to cover all kinds of protests. And that perception of nationalism, I think, of patriotism, is one that is deeply troubling to me as an obstruction to free speech and free association with one another.

Interviewer: Much of *Absolute Friends* has to do with spying in, against, and for the late, and largely unlamented, state of East Germany.

le Carré: Yes. And rightly unlamented: a terrible little state.

Interviewer: And a state which posed people with all sorts of dilemmas about loyalty and about how one reconciled one's own integrity with one's position in society; certainly a far cry from what the Englishman, Ted Mundy, faces in reconciling himself with his country.

le Carré: Yes. Both of these characters, the Brit and the German, come from shattered families and they are the inheritors of terrible pieces of history. On the one hand, the Englishman comes out of colonial India. His father was a creature of that imperial period in Britain. And my Englishman feels a little bit ashamed of that inheritance, as indeed I do. My German—his background is hideously complicated. It turns out, gradually, that his father was what was called in Hitler's time "Deutsche Christen." That was a Nazi Christian, in effect; a member of the tolerated Lutheran Church under Nazidom. He later changed his spots and became a Communist and, in the perception of his son Sasha, was an absolutely appalling and unintelligible man.

Both of them, therefore, are trying to achieve what we're all trying to achieve. That is a destiny which is not determined by their origins. And that's what unites them as friends. But at the same time, it dooms them.

Interviewer: Do you consider yourself a man with very, very close friendships, or with a very close friendship, as intense as the one you write about in this book?

le Carré: I've been through them at one time or another. I don't think that I have any close friendship now that has endured, but you know, at my age, one's friends die off. I think that I can look back, perhaps nostalgically, on people I've worked closely with and people with whom I shared great moments and terrible moments in my life. But I have no persistent friendship that would mirror the friendship that I've described in the novel, no.

Interviewer: I want to ask you about something else you've written recently, which is autobiographical, the story of your father and of your childhood. And your father was—he was a con man who spent time in prison.

le Carré: Yes, right.

Interviewer: And for those of us who read *A Perfect Spy*, we'll recall that the character Magnus Pym—his father was a conman, a fictive whitewash compared to what you actually write about in your own life, I might say. [le Carré laughs.] What a dreadful relationship with your father.

le Carré: Well, it's a quotation that I love from Graham Greene, that childhood is the bank balance of the novelist, the credit balance. And it may have been a dreadful relationship, but to grow up around somebody like that, as exotic, as truthless, and as affectionate as that, and to watch with a child's eyes how he would set up a mark and rip him off, or her off, and then, like Don Giovanni, always believe the last thing he had said and while he was saying it, believe it passionately and religiously; it was an extraordinary education, if you like.

And in deceit. I think it was Talleyrand who said that loyalty is about dates—when you believe in something, when you don't. And the ground shifts all the time. And with my father, the ground always shifted. As I grew up and my eyes got clearer, I realized what I was watching.

Interviewer: Nothing prepares one for a life of creating fiction like being raised in the fictitious universe created by one's father.
le Carré: I think that's true. I think that the one thing that marks most writers is the condition of unhappiness and alienation. I went to my first boarding school at the age of five. And growing up, on the one hand, in these weird, closed societies with archaic laws and built-in injustice and, on the other hand, living on—up and down with my father's fortunes in the holidays—I think it just drove me in upon myself and made the fictitious world the real one for me, the imaginative world that was a refuge that I could retreat to when life became incomprehensible.

Interviewer: I'm thinking of what Talleyrand said, what you just quoted about dates.
le Carré: Yes.

Interviewer: At what date did life cease being incomprehensible to you?
le Carré: Oh, I think I may safely say that has never happened.

Interviewer: Well. . . .
le Carré: I still find it a mystery. At my age, it's watching the movie come 'round again. I think the fact that after we had ended the Cold War, that we set about demonizing Islam, that we set about preparing ourselves for unlimited wars in the future; I continue to find that deeply depressing. And I suppose that's what I was fighting against in *Absolute Friends* and that, for as

long as I can, is what I will continue to fight against. I would long for more comprehension and a greater respect for the victims of our dreams.

Interviewer: Well, David Cornwell, John le Carré, thank you very much for talking with us once again.
le Carré: Thank you very much, Robert.

Interviewer: Mr. Cornwell is the author most recently of the novel *Absolute Friends*, under his pen name, John le Carré.

Index